Ten Steps to
Educational Reform
Making Change Happen

Robert H. Palestini

The Scarecrow Press, Inc.
Technomic Books
Lanham, Maryland, and London
2000

SCARECROW PRESS, INC.
Technomic Books

Published in the United States of America
by Scarecrow Press, Inc.
4720 Boston Way, Lanham, Maryland 20706
http://www.scarecrowpress.com

4 Pleydell Gardens, Folkestone
Kent CT20 2DN, England

British Library Cataloguing in Publication Information Available

Library of Congress Cataloging-in-Publication Data
Palestini, Robert H.
    Ten steps to educational reform : making change happen /
Robert H. Palestini.
    p. cm.
    Includes bibliographical references (p.) and index
    ISBN 0-8108-3864-8 (alk. paper)—ISBN 0-8108-3917-2 (paper : alk. paper)
    1. Educational change. 2. School improvement programs. 3. Educational planning
I. Title: 10 steps to educational reform.   II. title.
LB2822.8 .P24   2000
371.2'07—dc21   00-056344

♾™ The paper used in this publication meets the minimum requirements of
American National Standard for Information Sciences—Permanence of
Paper for Printed Library Materials, ANSI/NISO Z39.48–1992.
Manufactured in the United States of America.

Contents

Introduction
1

Chapter 1: Establishing a Climate for Change
8

Chapter 2: Assessing a Need
20

Chapter 3: Creating a Sense of Urgency
32

Chapter 4: Assessing Favorable and Opposing Forces
39

Chapter 5: Selecting Alternatives
57

Chapter 6: Promoting Ownership
71

Chapter 7: Providing Staff Development
81

Chapter 8: Operationalizing Change
88

Chapter 9: Evaluating Change
103

Chapter 10: Institutionalizing Change
110

Chapter 11: Schoolwide Reform Models
114

Appendix A
132

Appendix B
141

Index
151

About the Author
153

Introduction

Education, particularly urban public education, seems to be in a continual state of crisis. None of its constituencies seems to be satisfied with its outcomes. There is no dearth of remedies, however. Educational research has produced a variety of reforms that the scholars claim will resolve many of the problems encountered in American education. Until now, however, the major problem has been how to implement these reforms effectively. There have been sporadic successes, but generalizing from these effective models has been problematic.

Reforms such as site-based management, charter schools, clustering, whole language instruction, cooperative learning, and outcomes-based education all have their advocates. Pilot programs using these approaches have proved successful. The frustration lies in how to implement these reforms universally so that the schools where they are effective become the rule rather than the exception. In a nutshell, the issue becomes: how do we successfully effect change?

Human instinct seems to prefer the status quo. Intellectually, however, we all seem to realize that to progress, we need to experience change. Collectively, we have bought into Edwards Deming's notion that for any institution to thrive, "continuous improvement" is an absolute necessity. And continuous improvement implies change. But none of this rationalizing makes it any easier to accept. When dealing with the process of change, we seem to operate on a visceral level. Our security need seems to militate against any sort of significant change. Nevertheless, if our schools and school districts are to progress, we need to overcome our instincts and implement the reforms that will make them effective in educating our young people.

In an earlier work, *The Ten-Minute Guide to Educational Leadership*, I suggest that if the educational leader systematically focuses on ten aspects or his or her institution each day, that administrator will be effective.[1] These ten components include the school's organizational structure, its organizational climate, leadership, motivation, communication, planning, decision-making and conflict management processes, power distribution, and attitude toward change. Of these essential elements, I believe that an institution's tolerance of and ability to change is the most important element for success. I also believe that mastering the ability to effect change successfully to transform an institution is the culminating activity of the effective educational leader.

Successfully effecting change requires the educational leader to have mastered all of the other elements necessary for promoting organizational effectiveness. To effect successful change, the educational administrator must have outstanding leadership skills, ensure that the organizational structure is appropriate, engender a climate of trust and respect, motivate his or her colleagues to achieve a vision, communicate effectively, plan strategically, incorporate appropriate decision-making techniques, effectively manage conflict, and empower faculty and staff. This is a daunting task—so daunting that the average educational administrator is not able to cope with it. As a result, successful implementation of change in the form of educational reform remains the exception rather than the rule; and effective schools remain the exception rather than the rule.

An Integrated Approach to Change

The literature is replete with various suggested change processes. Many of them contain elements that are helpful in leading to successful transformation, but none contains all of the necessary elements. As a result, through the process of trial and error, I have developed my own process for change. It is termed an *integrated change process* because although there are distinct steps in the process, the key to their successful implementation is that many of them are implemented simultaneously rather than sequentially.

The ten steps I am suggesting are these:

- Establishing a climate for change
- Assessing a need
- Creating a sense of urgency
- Assessing favorable and opposing forces
- Selecting alternatives
- Promoting ownership
- Providing staff development
- Operationalizing change
- Evaluating change
- Institutionalizing change

Most attempts at effecting change in the form of educational reform fail because leaders have no plan at all or do not engage in all of the steps in the process. Other failures occur when administrators try to implement the reform by following the change process steps sequentially rather than simultaneously and get bogged down in one or another of the steps, unable to bring the process to closure.

The Washington School

Suppose the mythical Washington School received a mandate to introduce site-based management, whose objective was to empower a team of faculty and staff to assist the administration in the operation of the school. And suppose the principal, Rita Curran, had operated the school successfully in a relatively autocratic manner for the past ten years. The faculty leader of the site-based management team was Jodi Jones, who felt that giving the staff a voice in decision making was long overdue.

How would the Washington School move toward site-based management? What changes are required? Who will implement them? What resistances will they face? These are a few of the questions that need to be posed and answered if the Washington School is to move successfully toward site-based management. To bring about this change effectively, a model of planned change needs to be engaged.

The model of planned change suggested here includes ten steps that reflect a systematic approach to introducing a school reform such as site-based management. The first step in the process is to establish a positive climate for change in the Washington School. For this particular change to be accepted, the groundwork has to be laid so that the faculty and staff are comfortable with the notion of change. Rita Curran, the principal, has to model her own tolerance and acceptance of change. She has to encourage change in the past and engage in change so that it becomes almost routine. Even superficial change, such as painting the school lockers a different color, or varying teacher rosters every two or three years, can foster a positive climate toward change.

So change begins by obtaining information about those involved in the change situation. In particular, the person(s) responsible for making the changes or for ensuring that they occur must assess the organization's readiness for change, including consideration of the environment in which it functions and the nature of its workforce. In the case of the Washington School, Rita Curran, Jodi Jones, and the others involved in site-based management must assess the organization before implementing the new form of administration. They might consider, for example, how the various members of the faculty and staff will react when given the news that such a significant change is taking place. They might want to collect data on the workforce's openness to change. If they have done their jobs of nurturing a climate for change, one hopes they will find that their faculty and staff are ready.

While the school climate is being assessed to determine if the faculty and staff are ready for this change, Rita Curran must identify a need in the school for site-based management. Ordinarily, such a need assessment is conducted before the change or reform required is identified. However, in this case, that luxury is not available. This change has been mandated from above, and Rita must cope with it. This is unfortunate but not uncommon in our educational institutions. In Rita's favor, however, is the fact that she has operated the school in a somewhat arbitrary manner in the past. Thus, there will be a certain openness to this type of change. Rita should take advantage of this opportunity to identify the need for more faculty and staff prefer input in decision making. In effect, she is identifying a reason for the change—a justification for the reform.

In the next step, the change agent(s) attempts to create a sense of urgency for the change. In this case, Rita Curran and her colleagues must make the argument that if the change to site-based management does not take place, dire circumstances will result. Rita might point out that remaining with the status quo may result in continued inefficiencies, student achievement declines, and enrollment decreases. Ultimately, the continued existence of the Washington School will be in jeopardy. Unfortunately, only when such alarming circumstances are raised are educational institutions spurred to action.

The fourth step is perhaps the most important one in the integrated change process. Here we consider the forces affecting the change. It is during this phase that a force field analysis can be helpful in identifying the forces in favor of the change and those opposed to it. After identifying these forces, the change agent(s) should engage in the interventions necessary to enhance the forces in favor of site-based management and mitigate the forces against it. For example, Jodi Jones, the faculty representative, has already demonstrated a proclivity for site-based management, seeing it as "long overdue." Her attitude toward the change should be cultivated by reinforcing her interest, perhaps by appointing her as the "faculty champion" of site-based management. On the other hand, the principal, Rita Curran, would seem to be opposed to the change. After all, she was comfortable with operating the school in "a relatively autocratic manner for the last ten years." Perhaps the superintendent should ask Rita to visit another school where site-based management has been used successfully. With interventions such as this Rita may be convinced to be an active and effective agent of change.

During the next phase, the change agent(s) generate alternative strategies for meeting the objectives of the change. They outline the prescription for change; determine the steps needed to implement it; and detail the nature, cost, timing, and personnel required for any new system. This step also requires the change agent(s) to integrate the activities of the previous step in anticipating and planning for all possible consequences of the change effort.

Promoting a sense of employee ownership of the change is of major importance. This should be integrated into all of the steps, but it is mentioned as a separate step to give it emphasis. The more people involved in the process, the better. Where possible, input from inside and outside the school should be obtained. When this type of involvement occurs, a sense of ownership is more likely to be established, and, consequently, it is more likely that the change will be accepted.

An often overlooked step in the process of change is the need for staff development. It would be disastrous if Rita Curran and Jodi Jones attempted to implement site-based management without being trained themselves, and, just as important, without their staffs being trained. Without a thorough understanding of the substance of any significant educational reform and its implications, dire consequences can and will occur.

Operationalizing the change involves placing it into action. In this phase, the change agent(s), Jodi Jones, Rita Curran, other faculty and administration, parents, top administrators in the school system, and others, implement the best strategies that arise out of the planning phase.

During the evaluation phase, the change agent(s) collects data about the nature and effectiveness of the change as it occurs. The results of the evaluation indicate whether the change process is complete or a return to an earlier stage is needed. The criteria for success should be specified in advance of a change effort; these criteria may be culturally linked and varied. If the introduction of site-based management results in ineffective outcomes, the process should return to an earlier stage—for example, needs assessment—to determine if the school really needs this change; or assessing forces, to determine if enough of the staff has been convinced of the need for site-based management; or the planning phase, to determine if the best strategies for meeting the objectives were chosen. Ultimately, however, if site-based management proves to be ineffective at the Washington School, the decision to discontinue it is made during this stage.

The last step in the integrated change process is institutionalization. During this phase, plans for continuing the change into the future are specified. Successful changes should be institutionalized—that is, the changed processes should be established as permanent ways of operating; otherwise, when the present change agent(s) leaves, the change may not be perpetuated. Ideally, the change should become part of the school's organizational culture. Incorporating the principles of site-based management into the organizational chart and governance system of the Washington School and the school system is one way of institutionalizing this particular reform.

This text devotes a chapter to each of the steps of the integrated change process and describes in detail how it can best be carried out. To help the reader apply these ten change elements to a real-life situation, an actual case study involving initiation of an integrated language arts (ILA) program in a large, urban school system is used. ILA was a radical departure from a one-hundred-year tradition of using an exclusively phonics-based approach to language arts education, so it truly constituted a transformational or structural change, which is the most difficult type of educational reform to effect. In addition, educators are very busy people, so a diagnostic checklist appears at the end of each chapter that encapsulates the points made in the text.

Endnote
1. Robert H. Palestini, *The Ten-Minute Guide to Educational Leadership* (Lancaster: Technomic Publishing, 1998).

1

Establishing a Climate for Change

Keep changing. When you're through changing, you're through.
— Bruce Barton

E. Mark Hanson, in his text titled *Educational Administration and Organizational Behavior*, describes an incident regarding the process of change. Always interested in the processes of school improvement, he once asked the superintendent of a large, urban school district, "How does change come about around here?" She thought for a moment. "Well," she replied, "there is the normal way and the miraculous way. The normal way," she continued, "is where the heavens part and the angels come down and do the change for us. The miraculous way is when we do it ourselves."[1]

Articulating the Need for Change

At your institution, change should be expected. It should be perceived as something positive and routine. The need for change in the context of continuous improvement should be articulated constantly by institutional leaders. College presidents, superintendents, and principals should set the tone for change by taking every opportunity to articulate its necessity and model it in their own leadership. For example, the annual faculty convocation can be the occasion for articulating the notion that if the institution is to progress, academically and operationally, it must be open to change. The possible changes that are anticipated during the upcoming school year can be shared. At subsequent faculty meetings, the need for change can be reinforced.

Modeling Change

In addition to articulating the need for change, to promote a positive school climate the leader must model a tolerance for change. Even if it is something simple, such as changing the color of the school lockers every two or three years or changing the format of faculty meetings to incorporate innovative concepts like cooperative learning and shared decision making, the leader needs to lead by example. The leader must be perceived as being open to new ideas and providing a climate in which creativity is fostered.

While fostering a climate for change, the leader must be careful not to be perceived as being in favor of change for its own sake. If this occurs, it can have a counterproductive or dysfunctional effect. One way of precluding such a perception is to establish with your staff the basics or essentials of your institution—the things that are constant and do not change—and those that must change for your institution to remain healthy. Such fundamentals as academic excellence, individual attention, community involvement, and an emphasis on educational outcomes might be identified as remaining constant, while instructional methods, curricular approaches, and organizational structure are subject to change.

Another way to avoid being perceived as in favor of change for change's sake is to be certain that when a change is implemented, all of the steps in the process are followed. If this is done, it is more likely that the change will be implemented successfully in the first place, and, second, if the change is not effective, the evaluation stage of the process provides an opportunity to move away from it gracefully. In addition, success breeds success. If the leader has a record of implementing change successfully, it paves the way for future change. If leaders also have a reputation for objectively evaluating the effectiveness of the change and abandoning it if it is unsuccessful, they will foster a climate with a high tolerance for change.

Trust and Respect

If a positive climate for change is to be established, another requisite is an environment of trust and respect. Institutions do not amount to anything without the people who make them what they are. The individuals most influential in making institutions what they are, are essentially volunteers. Our very best teachers and administrators can work anywhere they please. So, in a sense, they volunteer to work where they do. As educational leaders, we would do far better if we looked on and treated our employees as volunteers. To engender trust and respect, therefore, we should treat our employees as if we had a covenantal rather than a contractual relationship with them.[2]

If an educational institution is to be a place where change is not only tolerated, but embraced, it must be successful in creating a culture of trust and respect so that everyone in it feels as if he or she "owns the place." "This is not the school district's school; it is not the board of education's school; it is my school." Taking ownership is a sign of one's love for an institution. In his book, *Servant Leadership*, Robert Greenleaf says, "Love is an undefinable term, and its manifestations are both subtle and infinite. It has only one absolute condition: unlimited liability!"[3] Although it may run counter to our traditional notion of American capitalism, employees should be encouraged to act as if they "own the place"; it is a sign of love, and it is a prerequisite for establishing a positive climate for change.

The Cycle of Change

Projecting change as a cyclical rather than a linear process is another way of creating a climate that tolerates change. Recognizing the change imperative is followed by developing a shared direction, implementing the change, consolidating it, and sustaining it. But the process does not stop at that point. The process should be perceived as cyclical in that the very outcome of the change is often the stimulus for additional change. Thus, the unending process continues. The final stage of the change cycle always contains the seeds of the next cycle. One of the most vital responsibilities of the leader is to resist being lulled into a sense of complacence by the fruits of successful change and be vigilant for the signs for new areas of change.

Change Facilitator Behaviors

Establishing a climate for change can be facilitated if the leader(s) engages in behaviors that promote change. Certain behaviors by school principals have been identified as facilitating change.[4] The data are drawn from actual research comparing more and less effective principals involved in school improvement. It identifies effective principal behaviors in the following areas:

- Vision
- Structuring the school as a workplace
- Structuring involvement with change
- Sharing responsibility
- Decision making
- Guiding and supporting
- Structuring their professional roles

Vision

The principal who facilitates change is one who, rather than accepting district goals as school goals, respects district goals but insists on goals for his or her school that give priority to the local school's student needs. Further, the principal takes initiative in identifying future goals and priorities for the school and in preparing to meet them. Rather than simply responding to teachers', students', and parents' interests in the goals of the school and the district, the principal establishes a framework of expectations for the school and involves others in setting goals within that framework.

Structuring the School as a Workplace

Rather than maintaining a low profile in the day-to-day operation of the school, the change facilitator directs the ongoing operation of the school with emphasis on instruction through personal actions and a clear designation of responsibility. He or she sets standards and expects high performance levels from teachers, students, and self. His or her first priority is the instructional program; personnel and collaborative efforts are directed at supporting that priority. This principal insists that everyone involved with the school give priority to teaching and learning, and establishes, clarifies, and models norms for the school.

Structuring Involvement with Change

The change facilitator seeks out information from teachers, district personnel, and others to gain an understanding of the innovation and changes required for improvement, rather than relying on information provided by other change facilitators from outside the school. These principals accommodate district expectations for change and push for adjustments and additions that will benefit their schools. They direct the change process in ways that lead to effective use by all teachers and staff. They give teachers specific expectations and steps regarding application of the change. They monitor the change effort through classroom observation, review of lesson plans, reports that reveal specific teacher involvement, and specific attention to the work of individual teachers. Finally, they give direct feedback to teachers about what they learned through monitoring, which includes a comparison with expected behaviors and a plan for next steps.

Sharing Responsibility

Rather than allowing others to assume the responsibility for the change effort, these leaders delegate to carefully chosen others some of the responsibility for the change effort. Those chosen are likely to be from within the school to demonstrate the leader's confidence in his or her staff. Also, rather than allowing others to assume responsibility and have considerable autonomy and independence in which responsibilities they assume and how they carry them out, the change facilitator first establishes which responsibilities will be delegated and how they are to be accomplished, then works with others and closely monitors the carrying out of these tasks.

Decision Making

The change facilitator principal handles routine decisions through established procedures and assigned responsibilities to cut down on the required time for these tasks, rather than making these kinds of decisions at the last minute. Further, these leaders make decisions based on the standard of high expectations and what is best for the school as a whole, particularly learning outcomes and longer-term goals. Finally, change facilitators allow others to participate in decision making and delegate decision making to others within carefully established parameters of established goals and expectations. In current terminology, these leaders improve their effectiveness by empowering others, rather than wielding their own power.

Guiding and Supporting

Rather than believing that teachers are professionals and leaving them alone to do their work unless they request assistance or support, the change facilitator believes that teachers are responsible for developing the best possible instruction so expectations for their involvement with innovation is clearly established. These principals anticipate the need for assistance and resources and provide support as needed, and sometimes before problems arise. They collect and use information from a variety of sources to be aware of how the change effort is progressing, and plan interventions that will increase the probability of a successful, quality implementation. They provide additional knowledge or skills needed by the teachers through other personnel and resources within the building. They also provide direct programmatic support through interventions targeted to individuals and to the staff as a whole. Finally, they demand constant, effective implementation from the teachers.

Structuring Their Professional Roles

Here is where the change facilitator demonstrates the difference between a manager and a leader. The manager is content with maintaining the status quo—"keeping the trains running on time." The true leader sees his or her role as one of ensuring that the school has a strong instructional program with teachers teaching students so they are able to learn. Further, they identify areas that need improvement and initiate action for change. They sort through new ideas presented from within and outside the school and implement those deemed to have high promise for school improvement. They are concerned with how others view the impact of the school on students. They respect the rules of the district, but they determine their behavior by what is required for maximum effectiveness of their own schools. Other change-facilitating behaviors include keeping abreast of all that is going on in the school through direct contact with the classroom, individual teachers, and students; responding to others with concern but placing student priorities above all else; developing sufficient knowledge to be able to make specific teaching suggestions and troubleshoot any problems that may emerge; knowingly sacrifices the short-term feeling of staff if doing a task now is necessary for the longer-term goals of the school; and seeking teachers' ideas and reactions to the change facilitator's ideas, and then setting priorities.

The Change Facilitator Styles Inventory in appendix A should be of value in determining whether you are exhibiting the behaviors necessary for establishing a climate that will facilitate change.

The Congruence Model

David Nadler has captured the essence of establishing the culture for change in his book, *Champions of Change*.[5] He identifies six internal components of an organization that can promote a culture of change:

(a) individual–organization, (b) individual–task, (c) individual–informal organization, (d) task–organization, (e) task–informal organization, and (f) organization–informal organization. The greater the congruence among these internal components, the more effective organizations will be in transforming their strategies into performance. Conversely, the poorer the fit, the wider the gap between strategy and performance. For change agents about to embark on a significant change or reform, identifying the points at which the institution has congruence, or the lack thereof, is a vital step to the reform's ultimate success. Table 1.1 illustrates Nadler's six organizational components.

For anyone involved in planning or managing change, this model implies three general principles that can significantly affect success:

- *Be certain that the change fits the realities of the institution's resources and environment.* During economically and demographically good times, school districts and institutions of higher education often expand their infrastructures to accommodate the sudden influx of students without considering the long-range implications. When times are not so good, they are saddled with an infrastructure that can no longer be supported—thus, the proliferation of restructuring, right-sizing, and the like. If these institutions had not overexpanded in the first place, they would not be confronted with their current dilemmas.
- *Make certain that the reform fits the formal structures, systems, and processes of the institution.* For example, we argue that an integrated approach to change is the most effective one. Integration requires a flexible communication process whereby the lines are not strictly drawn. If a school has rigid expectations with regard to lines of communication, where one must adhere strictly to the "chain of command," the chance of successful change using the integrated approach is low. Either the communication process needs to be altered, or another change process needs to be used.

TABLE 1.1 / Meaning of Fit for Each Component

FIT	ISSUES
Individual–organization	To what extent individual needs are met by the organizational arrangements. To what extent individuals hold clear or disoriented perceptions of organizational structures; the convergence of individual and organizational goals.
Individual–task	To what extent the needs of individuals are met by the tasks; to what extent individuals have skills and abilities to meet task demands.
Individual–informal organization	To what extent individual needs are met by the information organization. To what extent the informal organization makes use of individual resources, consistent with informal goals.
Task–organization	To what extent organizational arrangements are adequate to meet the demands of the task; to what extent organizational arrangements tend to motivate behavior consistent with task demands.
Task–informal organization	To what extent the informal organization structure facilitates task performance; to what extent it hinders or promotes meeting the demands of the task.
Organization–informal organization	To what extent the goals, rewards, and structures of the informal organization are consistent with those of the formal organization.

We argue that the integrated approach is the most effective change model, so we would recommend the former.

- *Be certain that there is a fit among all the internal components of the institution—the change to be made, the organizational structure, the formal and informal organizational arrangements, and the people.* Do not assume that changing one or two components of the model will not affect the smooth functioning of the institution. For example, how many times have you seen well-intentioned administrators decide to change the site of the faculty lounge or dining room, or change the faculty parking location, only to find that their thinking was not in line with their constituency's—the result being utter chaos.

■ A CASE STUDY

The case study used throughout the text involves initiation of an integrated language arts (ILA) program in grades K–6 in an urban/suburban school district of nearly 200 schools and 90,000 students. Since the school system dates back to the late 1800s, its culture was conservative and traditional one. The school system had experienced much success during its history, and its standardized test scores in reading and language arts had remained relatively high. Having experienced a degree of success, there was great resistance to any perceived threat to the status quo.

According to the integrated change process suggested here, the first step is to establish a positive climate for change. In the case of the ILA program, the positive climate for change was established in at least three basic ways. First, the need for change was articulated early and often. Second, a tolerance for change was modeled by those leaders ultimately responsible for inaugurating and implementing change. Third, and most important, an environment of trust and respect was established. Without trust and respect, no change can be implemented effectively. On the contrary, in an environment of trust and respect, even faulty planning can be made to work—a scary thought, indeed.

As early as two full years before the ILA program was suggested, the groundwork for such a significant systemwide change was being prepared. At various faculty meetings, convocations, and professional development sessions, Edwards Deming's principles of Total Quality Management were espoused, with primary emphasis on his notion that "continuous improvement" was a staple for the healthy institution. The point was made often that continuous improvement assumes change, and that academic institutions are no different from any other organizations in their need to respond to changing trends in the marketplace. Because of the almost instinctive reluctance to change, we established those principles that we considered to be the essence of our mission, and, therefore, not subject to change. Such fundamentals as a belief that all children can achieve; the family provides the foundation for the development of the individual; expectation influences achievement; education is vital to a strong, healthy community; a safe, positive learning environment is crucial to education; quality education empowers an individual to achieve potential; students learn at different rates and in different times, and service to others were identified as core values that would not be altered. However, almost everything else was considered to be incidental and, therefore, subject to change. So the need for a positive view of change had been articulated clearly.

At the same time that we were articulating the need for change, we set about our efforts to model a tolerance for change. We implemented a number of more minor changes to improve the education and services provided to students. The physical education program was reemphasized in the newly developed culture of increased physical activity to provide physical exercise for all students at the same time. A *Ten at Ten* program was developed whereby all students in the system performed ten specially designed cardiovascular exercises for ten minutes at exactly ten o'clock in the morning. We also partnered with the National Diffusion Network to expose our faculty to educational innovations from across the nation. Exposure to these innovative methods and techniques was provided to the faculty at a local university during the summer. In all of the changes faculty input was sought and obtained and all of the steps suggested in the integrated change process were followed closely. Thus, we modeled a healthy attitude toward change.

True to our emphasis on an integrative approach to change, at the same time that we were articulating the need to change and modeling a tolerance for change, we set about establishing an environment of trust and respect. We developed the change indicated above with major input and full approval of the faculty, staff, and parents in each of the schools. Students were also integrally involved in the change process. The objectives of each change were clearly articulated and understood. Care was taken to be certain that equity and fairness prevailed. A sense of goodwill on the part of every constituency was established. Long-range goals were not sacrificed for short-term successes. In other words, we were not about making certain individuals look good, or making a name for themselves. Our clear focus was on meeting the changing needs of our customers, the students, and providing for the long-range good health of our school system. Since we had earned the trust and respect of our constituencies, clearly articulated the need for change in general, and modeled a tolerance for change, in effect, we had established a positive climate for change that would prove invaluable in the final outcome of the ILA program. The first step in the integrated change process had been accomplished.

Diagnostic Checklist

Here are a few questions that you can address in assessing your institution's climate for change:

1. Is the need for change being *articulated* constantly?
2. Is the institution's leadership *modeling* change?
3. Is a climate of *trust and respect* being nurtured?
4. Are the leaders engaging in effective *change behavior*?

Endnotes

1. E. Mark Hanson. *Educational Administration and Organizational Behavior* (Boston: Allyn and Bacon, 1991). p. 300.
2. Max de Pree, *Leadership Is an Art* (New York: Dell Publishing, 1989).
3. Ibid., p. X (AU: Pls supply)
4. Thomas J. Sergiovanni, *Schooling for Tomorrow* (Boston: Allyn and Bacon, 1989).
5. David A. Nadler, *Champions of Change* (San Francisco: Jossey-Bass, 1998).

2

Assessing a Need

> The problem is not therefore, to suppress change,
> which cannot be done, but to manage it.
> — Alvin Toffler

The next step in the integrated change process is the needs assessment. Unfortunately, this step is often ignored. Many educational leaders become enamored of one educational reform or another and try to implement it whether or not there is an identified need. Reforms such as the whole language approach to reading, cooperative learning, block scheduling, interdisciplinary curricula, and even site-based management have been adopted arbitrarily by misguided educational administrators. When implemented without a needs assessment, or at least an after-the-fact needs assessment, these changes are destined to failure.

Ordinarily a needs assessment calls for a review of existing data and may require some surveying of clients and other appropriate reference groups. There is always a certain risk in a needs assessment. In the process of uncovering needs, one may also raise expectations that all of the respondent's concerns will be addressed. Fundamental to effecting change is priority setting and focus; thus, not all needs can be met immediately. Resources are in short supply, and difficult, sometimes painful decisions have to be made about which an array of critical needs requires attention.

Three reference groups are especially important to the needs assessment and the change process: students and parents, professional staff, and educational policy makers.

Students and Parents

Data about students are readily available in the records a typical school generates and maintains. Standardized test scores, attendance records, free or reduced-price lunch recipients, analyses of students with disabilities, transportation reports, and a host of other official and unofficial sources serve as basic data sources when it comes time to develop a profile of the students in the school or school district. Informal discussions with colleagues, other professionals, and parents and community members about how former students are doing is another source of information. Systematic observation by both teachers and administrators is still another way of assessing whether there is a need for change in the school.

Use of community and parent surveys can be very helpful to the school principal, as can community advisory groups. Such surveys are invaluable in determining parent and community expectations and attitudes and perceptions of educational needs of the community's young people. The diverse nature of most communities requires that in any survey care needs to be taken that the necessary degree of randomness exists. Concern for complete information and diversity of opinion should also be reflected in the composition of advisory groups.

Professional Staff

Another source of information regarding the needs of the school is the professional staff. They can be helpful with regard to instructional and curricular needs and can offer specific observations about the nature of the student body. Staff surveys or any of a number of rational problem-solving processes are useful in needs assessments. Using some of these methods in combination can be effective. For example, a faculty meeting may be used to brainstorm the strengths and weaknesses of the institution. The information could then be summarized and items generated for a survey to determine the perceived intensity and importance of the issues identified. The nominal group technique or the Delphi technique, both depicted in figure 2.1 , can then be used.

Educational Policy Makers

Central office personnel, local and state board members, state departments of education, legislators, the federal Department of Education, education advocacy groups, and other such entities are examples of educational policy makers. They also should be consulted to identify the needs of the educational institution.

Developing a Needs Assessment Instrument

A needs assessment instrument can be created by using the mission or belief statement of the educational entity as a base. A series of items that can be rated on a five-point Likert-type rating scale, ranging from strongly disagree to strongly agree, can be developed for each objective in the mission or belief statement. An illustration of a needs assessment statement is as follows:

	SA	A	N	DA	SD
Opportunities for shared decision making are provided to the faculty and staff.	1	2	3	4	5

Items can be grouped into logical categories, weighted, and scored. For example, if belief statements are organized around concepts from the effective schools research findings regarding curriculum, instruction, leadership, and assessment, then several items could be written for each of these categories. Responses can be divided by the number of items in the category in order to be viewed equally. This will allow a comparison between categories for later priority determination. Exhibit 2.1 on pages 25 and 26 gives a complete illustration of a needs assessment instrument, including a weighted scoring sheet

FIGURE 2.1 / (A) Steps in Nominal Grouping. (B) Steps in the Delphi Technique.

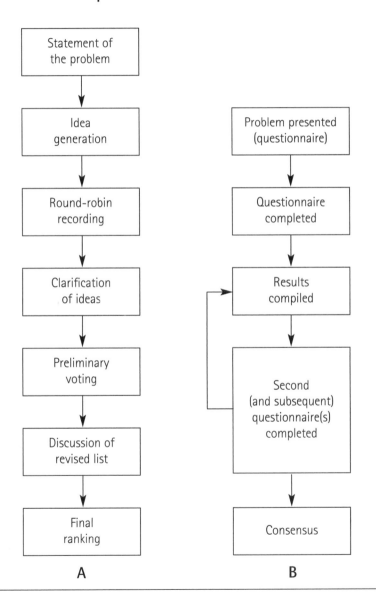

that is organized around effective schools concepts.

Beginning in the 1970s, the effective schools movement took school districts across the country by storm. Effective schools researchers were attempting to respond to public that was dissatisfied with the nation's schools, particularly inner-city schools. In short, the basic messages of these researchers were (a) schools can and do make a difference in the intellectual development of students, even under adverse conditions, and (b) by duplicating the inner workings of schools that have managed to rise above normal expectations, any school can effect positive change by refocusing its energies and resources.

Effective schools researchers have produced numerous lists of educational characteristics that they argue produce higher test scores. More often than not, certain features are repeated among these lists:

- strong administrative leadership
- clear objectives
- a safe and orderly school environment
- test–curriculum alignment
- close monitoring of pupil progress
- coordination of instruction
- high expectations[1]

The change agent would be wise to use the effective schools research findings in his or her development of the needs assessment instrument. Although the development of the needs assessment instrument should be a major responsibility of the change agent, other staff members should contribute to the process. Upon completion of the newly developed needs assessment instrument, it should be administered to all members of the school community, both internal and external. Appendix B includes a needs assessment survey that may prove helpful. It is entitled *Heart Smart* and is intended to identify organizational weaknesses in a school setting that need to be addressed.

EXHIBIT 2.1 / Needs Assessment Instrument

School Excellence Inventory

Directions—Rate the following items on a scale of 1 to 5 to reflect your opinion of your school. (1 = Low . . . 5 = High)

	(Low)				(High)
1. Students have favorable attitudes toward school and learning.	1	2	3	4	5
2. Student learning is frequently evaluated using curriculum-referenced materials.	1	2	3	4	5
3. The staff has high expectations for the students and adults with whom they work.	1	2	3	4	5
4. Student time on-task behavior is maintained at a high level because:					
a. A climate of order and discipline has been established.	1	2	3	4	5
b. Limited time is needed to maintain order.	1	2	3	4	5
c. Classroom management tasks have been "routinized" to to maximize available instructional time.	1	2	3	4	5
d. The school staff has made a commitment to maximize learning time by reducing impediments to learning and interruptions of the school day.	1	2	3	4	5
5. Students and parents receive regular feedback regarding the student's progress.	1	2	3	4	5
6. Student attendance rates are high.	1	2	3	4	5
7. There is a clear understanding of what the school believes in and stands for, which includes:					
a. An academic focus.	1	2	3	4	5
b. A belief that all students have the ability to learn.	1	2	3	4	5
c. An expectation that each student will learn.	1	2	3	4	5
d. High expectations for each student.	1	2	3	4	5
8. Teachers regularly use techniques to ensure that all students are learning.	1	2	3	4	5
9. Staff members are evaluated regularly.	1	2	3	4	5
10. Programs and varied instructional techniques are provided to respond to each child's individual needs and differences.	1	2	3	4	5
11. Students feel valued and successful.	1	2	3	4	5
12. Individual help is provided to students when needed.	1	2	3	4	5
13. School staff members exhibit a high degree of concern and commitment for the achievement and well-being of each student.	1	2	3	4	5
14. The principal is effective because:					
a. He or she understands the process of instruction and accepts the responsibility for being an instructional leader.	1	2	3	4	5

continued

EXHIBIT 2.1 / Needs Assessment Instrument (continued)

	(Low)				(High)
b. He or she is an able manager.	1	2	3	4	5
c. He or she has high attainable expectations for the students and adults with whom he or she works.	1	2	3	4	5
d. He or she has goal clarity (a clear sense of purpose and priorities) and is able to enlist the support of others in understanding, accepting, and accomplishing those ends.	1	2	3	4	5
e. He or she recognizes the importance of (and actively involves) the people who work in and who are served by the school.	1	2	3	4	5
f. He or she assists the school staff in implementing sound instructional practices.	1	2	3	4	5
15. Students receive prompt feedback on their work.	1	2	3	4	5
16. Staff and student morale are high.	1	2	3	4	5
17. Members of the school staff are cooperative and supportive of each other.	1	2	3	4	5
18. The curriculum:					
a. Emphasizes mastery of basic skills.	1	2	3	4	5
b. Is well defined.	1	2	3	4	5
c. Is appropriately sequenced and articulated from grade to grade and from subject to subject.	1	2	3	4	5
d. Is evaluated regularly.	1	2	3	4	5
19. Techniques are used to pinpoint individual students' strengths and weaknesses.	1	2	3	4	5
20. The staff is competent and continues to grow and learn.	1	2	3	4	5
21. The school is open to and encourages participation and involvement by parents and other citizens.	1	2	3	4	5
22. Parents, students, and staff place a high priority on learning.	1	2	3	4	5
23. Students are instructed at the appropriate level of difficulty.	1	2	3	4	5

Summary Sheet — School Excellence Inventory

Time	Climate	Basic Commitment	Staff	Curriculum	Leadership	Evaluation
#4a = __	#1 = __	#7a = __	#3 = __	#10 = __	#14a = __	#2 = __
#4b = __	#6 = __	#7b = __	#9 = __	#18a = __	#14b = __	#5 = __
#4c = __	#11 = __	#7c = __	#13 = __	#18b = __	#14c = __	#8 = __
#4d = __	#16 = __	#7d = __	#17 = __	#18c = __	#14d = __	#12 = __
Total = __	#21 = __	#22 = __	#20 = __	#18d = __	#14e = __	#15 = __
+4 = __	Total = __	Total = __	Total = __	#18e = __	#14f = __	#19 = __
	+5 = __	+5 = __	-5 = __	Total = __	Total = __	#23 = __
				+6 = __	+6 = __	Total = __
						+7 = __

Alternative Models

An alternative to developing one's own needs assessment instrument is to use existing surveys or generic measures such as the Organizational Climate Description Questionnaire, the Organizational Health Inventory, or the Pupil-Control Ideology Form, shown in figure 2.2.

An example of an existing survey is the institution's most recent accreditation report. For example, the most recent Middle States Evaluation contains a list of the institution's strengths and weaknesses. One need go no further to identify the school or school district's needs.

The Organizational Climate Description Questionnaire (OCDQ-RE) includes items regarding the principal and staff's behavior patterns and how they relate to the school climate. This questionnaire identifies needs that pertain to the school climate. The Organizational Health Inventory identifies areas of needed improvement regarding leadership, communication, decision making, conflict management, and employee motivation. The Pupil Control Ideology Form (PCI) determines whether classroom management or school discipline is a problem area. Using these instruments individually or in combination can prove to be invaluable in accurately assessing the needs of the school and school system.

The Garbage Can Model

Another alternative needs assessment model is the *garbage can model.*[2] In contrast to the more or less logical and systematic processes proposed earlier, the garbage can model emphasizes the unsystematic quality of much of the change that takes place in institutions. In an institution with unclear goals, uncertain means of achieving the goals, and changing participants in decision making, a diverse set of problems and solutions tend to be presented simultaneously. The change agent should recognize that nonrational decisions may occur. Sometimes decisions fit solutions to problems in a way that resolves the problem, removing both the problem and solution from further con-

FIGURE 2.2 / The Pupil-Control Ideology (PCI) Form

To operationalize the concept of the pupil-control orientation along the custodial–humanistic continuum, the Pupil-Control Ideology (PCI) form was developed by Willower, Eidell, and Hoy (1967). The PCI is a 20-item scale with five response categories for each item, ranging from strongly agree to strongly disagree. A sample of specific items follow:

- It is desirable to require pupils to sit in assigned seats during assemblies.
- Directing sarcastic remarks toward a defiant pupil is a good disciplinary technique.
- Pupils should not be permitted to contradict the statements of a teacher in class.
- Too much pupil time is spent on guidance and activities and too little on academic preparation.

THE SIX DIMENSIONS OF THE OCDQ-RE

	Description	Sample Items
	Principal's Behavior	
1. Supportive Behavior	Reflects a basic concern for teachers. The principal listens and is open to teacher suggestions. Praise is given genuinely and frequently, and criticism is handled constructively. Supportive principals respect the professional competence of their staffs and exhibit both a personal and a professional interest in each teacher.	The principal uses constructive criticism. The principal compliments teachers. The principal listens to and accepts teachers' suggestions.
2. Directive Behavior	Requires rigid, close supervision. Principals maintain close and constant control over all teacher and school activities, down to the smallest details.	The principal monitors everything teachers do. The principal rules with an iron fist. The principal checks lesson plans.
3. Restrictive Behavior	Hinders rather than facilitates teacher work. The principal burdens teachers with paperwork, committee requirements, routine duties, and other demands that interfere with their teaching responsibilities.	Teachers are burdened with busywork. Routine duties interfere with the job of teaching. Teachers have too many committee requirements.

FIGURE 2.2 / The Pupil-Control Ideology (PCI) Form (continued)

THE SIX DIMENSIONS OF THE OCDQ-RE

	Description	Sample Items
		Teachers' Behavior
4. Collegial Behavior	Supports open and professional interactions among teachers. Teachers are proud of their school, enjoy working with the colleagues, and are enthusiastic, accepting, and mutually respectful of the professional competence of their colleagues.	Teachers help and support each other. Teachers respect the professional competence of their colleagues. Teachers accomplish their work with vim, vigor, and pleasure.
5. Intimate Behavior	Reflects a cohesive and strong network of social support among the faculty. Teachers know each other well, are close personal friends, socialize together regularly, and provide strong support for each other.	Teachers socialize with each other. Teachers' closest friends are other faculty members at this school. Teachers have parties for each other.
6. Disengaged Behavior	Refers to a lack of meaning and focus to professional activities. Teachers are simply putting in time and are nonproductive in group efforts or team building; they have no common goal orientation. Their behavior is often negative and critical of their colleagues and the organization.	Faculty meetings are useless. There is a minority group of teachers who always oppose the majority. Teachers ramble when they talk at faculty meetings.

sideration. The researchers note that this matching often occurs at random, and they use the image of participants dumping problems and solutions into a garbage can to reflect how problems and solutions may be mixed together. If solutions and problems meet at the right time to make a change, a rational outcome or choice is made. Otherwise, no change results. Since solutions go in search of problems, the stream of problems must coincide with the stream of solutions for optimal changes to be made. More recent expansions of this model try to make the change agent a more explicit part of the action by citing him or her as able to take advantage of opportunities when problems and solutions match. For example, say a school system was in the process of restructuring as a result of enrollment declines, and was deciding how to best do so. Out of the blue, a farmer in the school district died, and his heirs decided to sell his 100 acres to a land developer, thus solving the school system's problem. This instance—where a problem and a solution randomly converged—is an example of the garbage can model in action.

■ A CASE STUDY

The need for a new language arts curriculum was identified by analyzing the school system's standardized test scores in language arts and related areas. Although the McGraw/Hill California standardized achievement test scores in language arts had not declined, they had plateaued in recent years. In a culture of continuous improvement, this situation was not acceptable.

In the midst of this period of test score stagnation, scholarly research indicated that an innovative approach to the teaching of reading, called the *whole language model*, was significantly more effective than the traditional phonetics approach. A related body of research indicated that children learned more effectively if they were more active in the teaching/learning process. Thus, we considered the possibility of combining a whole language and interactive learning approach as a solution to the leveling off of our reading and language arts test scores.

In addition to our own observations, the Middle States Accreditation Association's visits to our various schools indicated that our language arts curriculum needed examination and analysis. This observation was particularly noteworthy in that, as we all know, the Middle States Report is most often only a reflection of what the school community pointed out in its self-study. Thus, the school community recognized this weakness.

The Middle States Report prompted us to conduct a formal needs assessment among the schools to determine if improvement of the language arts program was a universally perceived need. The results of the needs assessment reinforced the school community's concerns in this area.

The needs assessment also indicated, however, that there was considerable resistance to change. There was legitimate concern that adopting a totally new approach to reading and language arts, such as the whole language model, would mean a decline in test scores. Many in the school community expressed a desire to leave well enough alone.

In anticipation of these legitimate concerns, we decided not to throw the baby out with the bath water, but to modify our views on the approach to take. After much consultation, we decided that instead of suggesting the substitution of the whole language to the traditional approach to reading, we would suggest an integrated model that would retain the strengths of the traditional approach, while supplementing it with the best principles of the whole language approach; thus, the birth of the Integrated Language Arts program.

Diagnostic Checklist

Here are a few questions you can address in assessing whether your institution has identified a need for change:

1. Have data been *collected* that indicate a need for change in your institution?
2. Has a formal or informal *needs assessment* taken place?
3. Did the needs assessment survey reflect the *mission and beliefs* of the institution?
4. Has the needs assessment corroborated the *anecdotal data*?
5. Has the need for the identified change been *promulgated* to the school community?

Endnotes

1. E. Mark Hanson, *Educational Administration and Organizational Behavior* (Boston: Allyn and Bacon, 1991).

2. Judith R. Gordon, *A Diagnostic Approach to Organizational Behavior*, 4th Edition (Boston: Allyn and Bacon, 1993).

3

Creating a Sense of Urgency

Keep constantly in mind in how many things you
yourself have witnessed change already. The universe is
change; our life is what our thoughts make it."
— Meditations, II

Since our natural instinct is to resist change, to effect a needed change, a sense of alarm or urgency often must be created. To overcome our innate sense of inertia, the dire consequences of remaining in the status quo need to be articulated and, sometimes, even exaggerated. There are a number of ways to create a sense of urgency, including citing comparable data and projected enrollment declines. But in creating a sense of urgency, the change agent must be aware that individuals and groups are often moved by dissimilar forces. In other words, what may cause a sense of urgency in one person, may not do so in another.

The Results of Stress

Creating a sense of urgency or stress can have both functional and dysfunctional outcomes. Whether stress takes a constructive or destructive course is influenced by the sociocultural context in which the stress occurs, because differences tend to exaggerate barriers and reduce the likelihood of conflict resolution. The issues involved also will affect the likely outcomes. Whether the individuals or groups have cooperative, individualistic, or competitive orientations toward stress will affect the outcomes, as well.

Effective educational administrators learn how to create functional conflict and manage dysfunctional conflict. They develop and practice techniques for diagnosing the causes and nature of stress and transform it into a productive force that fosters needed change in the institution. Many universities, for example, have healthy competition among their schools for recruitment of the most qualified students. This is an example of a functional sense of urgency or stress.

One can see, then, that some stress is beneficial. It can encourage organizational innovation, creativity, and adaptation. For example, a number of nonpublic school systems, and even some public ones, allow schools within the system to compete for the same students. This *open enrollment* or *public school choice* policy often spawns innovation and change in marketing techniques and, more important, in curriculum and instruction. In these cases, creating a sense of urgency can result in more employee enthusiasm and better decision making. The trick is to be able to create a sense of urgency without allowing it to become dysfunctional. This means that the change agent must know the stages of stress and when to intervene.

Stages of Stress

Understanding the nature of stress is helped by considering it as a sequence of stages. Regardless of the level of stress, an historical but still useful view of the progression of stress suggests that each episode proceeds through one or more of five possible stages: (1) latent, (2) perceived, (3) felt, (4) manifest, and (5) stress aftermath. By specifying the stage of conflict an administrator can determine its intensity and select the best strategies for managing it.[1]

Stress begins when conditions for conflict exists. Individuals or groups may have power differences, compete for scarce resources, strive for autonomy, have different goals, or experience different role pressures. These differences provide the foundation for tension and, ultimately, stress and alarm. Departments such as academic services and financial services frequently experience latent conflict because the goal of one department, registering as many students as possible, is sometimes in conflict with the goal of the other department, which is bill collection. Inherent differences in perceptions and attitudes often contribute to their relationship.

In the next stage individuals or group members know that stress exists. They recognize differences of opinion, incompatible goals or values, efforts to demean the other party or group, and implementation of opposing actions. If financial services needs to have the students' financial responsibilities satisfied before they can attend class, and the academic services department believes that the students have a right to an education regardless of their financial status, a state of perceived conflict or stress exists. Likewise, if a neighboring school district has been very successful in obtaining government and private grants for its educational programs, while another district has been ineffectual in this area, a state of perceived stress or alarm exists.

In creating a sense of urgency, the change agent should be careful to intervene with the planned change at the perceived stage of stress development. At this stage the level of stress remains functional and positive, and the individual or group is most susceptible to accepting change. If the change agent allows the stress to advance to the *felt* or *manifest* stage, there is a danger that the sense of urgency will develop into dysfunctional conflict.

Intervention Points

The art of effecting successful change involves knowing when the appropriate degree of urgency has been created, and what factors will cause the proper degree of urgency in each individual or group. Knowing when the *perceived stage* has been reached is a matter of judgment. If the leader knows the needs and desires of his or her colleagues and coworkers, the timing of the intervention process will be more apt to be appropriate.

In addition to knowing when to intervene, the change agent must consider the factors that most likely will cause a sense of urgency in the various individuals and constituencies involved in the reform. For example, if a school district is considering adopting a whole language reading approach, the change agent might point out to the administrators that such a reform would make the district more competitive with neighboring school districts; whereas, when creating a sense of urgency with the faculty, the change agent might stress the instructional advantages of such an approach. When addressing the school board, one might point out that parents expect such a change. Or when dealing with the teachers' union, the change agent can stress that the change will ensure job security.

The point here is that knowing the needs and aspirations of the individuals and groups that make up the school community is helpful in creating this sense of urgency. Knowing what buttons to push will facilitate the process and increase the chances of success. A simple and effective procedure for identifying these needs is to make up a list of the individuals and groups in your institutions and determine an intervention that increases their sense of urgency.

The Success Syndrome

A number of educational institutions suffer from the *success syndrome*.[2] This condition is the result of a long history of achievement that results in a school earning the reputation of being "a school of excellence." The institution may even be formally recognized by the U.S. Department of Education as being *A School of Excellence*. Many times, the symptoms of the success syndrome are arrogance, complacency, insularity, and conservatism. The results of the syndrome are often decreased student focus, increased cost, loss of efficiency, less innovation, and an obsession with the status quo. The ultimate outcome of the syndrome is declining performance. Educational leaders should make every effort to prevent their institutions from contracting this dreaded disease.

Developing a Rationale for Reform

An effective method of creating a sense of urgency is the development of a rationale for the change or reform. One way of doing so is to develop a position paper. In considering any new program, one should address two basic questions: Should we do it? and Can we do it? The change agent should address these two questions in the position paper. If the answer to these two questions is yes, the change agent has made a compelling argument for faculty and community support of the change.

The first question—Should we do it?—can be divided into three additional questions:

- Does the reform complement the mission and beliefs of the institution?
- Is there a need in the community for the reform?
- Does the reform have academic integrity?

The educational leader should point out ways in which the reform specifically complements the mission of the institution. Next, the leader should present evidence of the need in the community for the reform. Finally, a case should be made that the academic integrity of the reform has been demonstrated in other institutions where it has been implemented.

The second, larger question is: Can we do it? In other words, does the institution have the material and human resources to implement the change successfully? Once again, the change agent needs to make a compelling argument that the resources are already or will be available to implement the reform. A carefully crafted position paper that effectively and convincingly addresses these questions helps create a sense of urgency for the suggested change.

■ A CASE STUDY

A sense of urgency for a reading and language arts program was established in a number of ways, and in different ways to different constituencies. The perceived stage of stress was reached by establishing a compelling need for the program. The results of the needs assessment indicating a strong desire for a program of this nature were disseminated to all factions of the school community. Since the standardized achievement test scores had begun to stabilize after a number of years of steady growth, an argument was made that only something like an ILA program would ensure the future academic good health of the school system programs. We also pointed out that the timing was critical in that our counterpart school systems were also in the process of developing new language arts programs, and that we wanted to retain our status as an excellent school system. Finally, we noted that the new language arts program would have a positive effect on the middle and high school programs. For example, we pointed out that reading and language arts were at the foundation of the learning process, so an improved model would enhance the entire K–12 educational program.

In addition to creating a sense of urgency by establishing a compelling need for a new and innovative approach to language arts, we used arguments that were particularly persuasive to our various constituencies. For example, when speaking to administrators, we emphasized how the ILA would put us in an advantageous position in the marketplace. When addressing faculty, we stressed the way in which the program fit within the mission of the school system and how it would facilitate learning. When speaking with parents and students, we argued that such an approach would prepare students better for the workplace and for higher education. In short, there was something in the ILA program for everyone, but the window of opportunity needed to be acted on immediately. Any delay would risk the loss of a once-in-a-lifetime opportunity to ensure the continued good health of the school system. In a nutshell, we had created a sense or urgency.

Diagnostic Checklist

Here are a few questions you can address in assessing whether a sense of urgency has been created:

1. Has the school community been taken to the *perceived stress stage*?

2. Have *compelling arguments* been developed for the reform?
3. Have they been applied to the appropriate *constituencies*?
4. Has a *position paper* on the reform been developed and distributed?

Endnotes

1. C. H. Coombs, The structure of conflict, *American Psychologist* 42(4) (1987): 355–63.

2. David A. Nadler, *Champions of Change* (San Francisco: Jossey-Bass, 1998), p. 56.

4

Assessing Favorable and Opposing Forces

One must never lose time in vainly regretting the
past nor in complaining about the changes which
cause us discomfort, for change is the very essence of life.
— Anatole France

In my experience, accurate assessment of the forces that affect proposed reform is the most important step in the integrated change
process. Correctly identifying the forces that favor the reform and
those that oppose it is crucial to effective implementation of the
change. Further, the interventions chosen to neutralize the forces
against and enhance the forces in favor are instrumental to its
eventual success.

Organizational Resistance to Change

The forces resistant to change can be considerable. These forces range
from simple ignorance of an individual to the complex vested interests
of our own institutions' members. As the comic strip character, Pogo,
phrased it, "We have met the enemy and he is us."

The forces resistant to change are an important part of the organization's environment or climate. They must be diagnosed, understood, and taken into account in the targeting process and in selecting
a change strategy. The environment harboring the forces of resistance

is typically not social or technical but sociotechnical. A sociotechnical interpretation of environment refers to the behavior of individuals as it is shaped by the interaction of technical characteristics such as instructional equipment, physical layout of the school, activity schedules, and social characteristics such as norms, informal groups, power centers, and the like. As Chin and Benne point out, "The problem-solving structures and processes of a human system must be developed to deal with a range of sociotechnical difficulties, converting them into problems and organizing the relevant processes of data collection, planning, invention, and tryout of solutions, evaluation and feedback of results, replanning, and so forth, which are required for the solution of the problem."[1]

Resistance to change occurs at the organizational level and the individual level. There is a high level of interaction between the two, and they cannot be separated completely. Resistance forces also differ among schools in terms of source, strength, and makeup. The forces presented here are by no means exhaustive, but do represent some of the major resistances.

The School as a Domesticated Organization

According to Richard Carlson, a major organizational feature that contributes to resistance to change is the domestication of public schools and other educational institutions.[2] A domesticated organization has many properties of the monopoly: it does not have to compete for resources, except in a very limited area; it has a steady flow of clients; and its survival is guaranteed. Although private schools and colleges do not possess all of these characteristics in the way that public schools do, many of their teachers view their institutions in this way. One often hears the college professor or the private school teacher proclaim in the light of declining enrollments, "That's the administration's problem."

Because these institutions are domesticated organizations, they do not face the problems of private organizations that make it necessary to build major change mechanisms into their structures. Change capability permits private organizations to make the necessary modifications in production and product continually to hold their share of the market and expand it if possible. The domestication of the school builds in a layer of protective insulation that cannot be penetrated easily.

An interesting example of this type of organizational behavior was part of California's omnibus educational reform bill of 1983, which was intended to increase instructional time in the classroom. A comparative study had shown that California's students received 2.5 weeks' less instructional time than the national average. The bill offered financial incentives to districts to meet the target of 180 days a year and 240 minutes a day at a cost of $250 million annually for the first three years. The average high school needed to add four days to its school year and six minutes each day to qualify for the incentive award of $75 per pupil. The average elementary school needed to add four days for a $55-per-pupil-per-day-bonus.

In light of a potential contract violation and teachers' resistance to increased instructional time without increased compensation, districts found creative ways to lengthen the school day and year without increasing instructional time. Some districts added one minute to each passing period between classes, which could add up to 900 minutes or about 18 50-minute classes. Other schools extended homeroom periods by 5 minutes each day, totaling 900 minutes per year. Others added an extra recess to the school day. Some schools did add one or two minutes of instructional time to each class.[3] When considering educational change in a domesticated organization, therefore, the result is not always the desired outcome.

The Resistance Cycle

Goodwin Watson points out that during the process of effecting change, perceived resistance moves through a four-stage cycle. He describes the arrival of a reform in these terms: "In the early stage, when only a few pioneer thinkers take the reform seriously, resistance appears massive and undifferentiated. 'Everyone' knows better; 'No one in his right mind' could advocate the chance. Proponents are labeled crack-pots or visionaries."[4]

In the second stage some support becomes evident, the pro and con forces become visible, and the lines of battle are drawn. In the third stage the battle is engaged "as resistance becomes mobilized to crush the upstart proposal." The supporters of the change are often surprised and frequently overwhelmed by the opposition's tenacity. Survival of the innovation depends on developing a base of power to overcome the opposition.

If the supporters of change are victorious in the third stage, the fourth stage is characterized by support flowing to the newly arrived reform. "The persisting resistance is, at this stage, seen as a stubborn, hide-bound, cantankerous nuisance. For a time, the danger of a counter-swing of the pendulum remains real."[5] The cycle begins anew when another effort toward change occurs.

Individual Resistance to Change

We have talked about types of organizational resistance to change. Now let us look at some individual resistances to change found in educational institutions. Any school administrator who attempts to effect an innovation usually encounters the vested interests that Hanson describes.

Once a program has been funded, the personnel who operate the program immediately acquire a strong vested interest in the perpetuation of the program. Their jobs are at stake. No matter how stupid or pointless the program may be, once a man accepts a job with it, he must proceed to bolster and defend his own personal decision, so he uses rhetoric to tell himself that his decision was, indeed, a wise decision.[6]

Another instance of educators allowing a vested interest to enter into resistance to change is when the change is a threat to their personal status; dissolves an informal group that is a source of personal satisfaction; is interpreted as a criticism of their personal performance;

increases their workload or responsibilities; or has been proposed by someone he or she dislikes or distrusts.

Another myth is that teachers and administrators are constantly searching for new and better ways to perform their tasks. March and Simon argue that ongoing "search behavior" is not representative of most people. Individuals begin to seek out new strategies only when they become dissatisfied with the present course of affairs. They write: "Individuals and organizations give preferred treatment to alternatives that represent continuation of present programs over those that represent change But this preference is not derived by calculating explicitly the costs of innovation or weighing these costs. Instead, persistence comes about primarily because the individual or organization does not search for or consider alternatives to the present course of action unless that present course is in some sense 'unsatisfactory.' The amount of search decreases as satisfaction increases."[7]

This argument implies that educators will not start a search for improvement unless some sort of feedback mechanism convinces them that present procedures are not working well, and the resulting anxiety compels them to look for a better way. An outsider or an insider trying to initiate change cannot simply convince a school of a better innovation based solely on its merits. They must also present data suggesting that an aspect of a current program needs improvement. In other words, one needs to create a sense of urgency, as indicated in chapter 3. Only then will concerned attention be adequately focused.[8]

Another individual resistance to change has its roots in the psychological systems of an individual. Some of the psychological forces generating tendencies toward resisting change are:

- *Habit.* A habit becomes established because the repetition of a specific behavior is satisfying. For example, an administrator may act continuously in an autocratic manner because the sense of power derived from this behavior is highly satisfying. This behavior thus becomes routinized.

- *Primacy.* When an individual first copes successfully with a task or problem, a persistent pattern of behavior often is established.
- *Selective perception and retention.* Once a belief has been established within an individual, a type of information screening takes place that tends to reinforce the attitude. Inservice teachers who go to graduate school, for example, often hear lectures on new instructional approaches, but conclude that it is just theory and will not work in practice.
- *Dependence.* Educators tend to have dependent relationships, as do all human beings. Whether stemming from parental attitudes, colleague expectations, or early reference groups, dependent relationships tend to constrain independent thought.
- *Insecurity and regression.* "The reaction of insecure teachers, administrators and parents, is, too often, to try to hold fast to the familiar or even to return to some tried-and-true fundamentals which typify the schools of the past."[9]

Resistance from Subordinates

Since the findings of the Hawthorne Effect (employee relationships affect production more than physical environment) studies, social scientists have begun to understand the nature and source of power that subordinates command.[10] From their positions of power in the "lowerarchy," in many instances subordinates can assume control of the organization's productive efforts by means of slowing down, speeding up, or striking. They also can become highly resistant to change.

Teachers often use their power to control events and to resist change. They may try to control change by subtle use of the pocket veto or by unsubtle demands shouted out at a board of education meeting. Through use of their power in the lowerarchy, teachers can strongly support change initiatives and resist them.

To indicate that resistance to change is inherently bad, however, is to suggest that all change is inherently good. Of course, neither is the case. Earlier views of teacher resistance suggested an almost irrational reaction to change initiatives based on such characteristics as habit, fear of the unknown, or unwillingness to take risks.[11]

Rossman, Corbett, and Firestone point out, however, that resistance is often a "rational defense against poorly planned and executed innovations."[12] Resistance is often a rational message communicated upwardly that the intended change is attacking the wrong problem, has not been adequately thought out, or perhaps has insensitively overloaded the staff with too much additional work.

For example, take the introduction of daily journal writing into a high school curriculum. A proposal that requires all students to write something every day sounds reasonable, even laudable. However, Albert Shanker points out the potential dangers of not thinking these things out.

The average high school teacher has 5 classes a day with 30 to 35 students in each—a total of at least 150 papers to read and grade for each writing assignment. If he or she spends just 5 minutes reading each paper and another 5 minutes making comments, the total time expended adds up to at least 25 hours a week for one assignment! Added to the enormous amount of normal preparation time needed for daily lessons, an effective, continuing (journal) writing program is simply impossible.[13]

For school administrators, the study of resistance to change should be viewed as a learning experience. It focuses on and clarifies informal goals, priorities, and motives of many individuals close to the students. Reforms are often far better when implemented for having gone through the process.

Force Field Analysis

To understand the changing forces that affect a change, we can use an analytical technique called *force field analysis*, which views a problem as a product of forces working in different, often opposite directions. An organization, or any of its subsystems, maintains the status quo when the sum of opposing forces is zero. When forces in one direction exceed forces in the opposite one, the organization or subsystem moves in the direction of the greater forces. For example, if forces for change exceed forces against change, then change is likely to occur.

To move the educational institution toward a different desired state requires increasing the forces for change in that direction, decreasing the forces against change in that direction, or both. Generally, reducing resistance forces creates less tension in the system and fewer unanticipated consequences than increasing forces for change. At the Washington School, for example, reducing the resistances to the changes created by the introduction of site-based management increases the likelihood of the changeover. Figure 4.1 shows what happens when a resistance force is eliminated. When the administrators and staff no longer resist change, the present state, as shown by the solid vertical line, moves closer to the desired state, as indicated by the broken vertical line. A complete analysis looks at ways to alter all forces, for and against change.

Consider again the situation at the Washington School. Site-based management focused on changing school governance to include greater participation by more diverse constituencies. It meant removing some control from the school principal and other top administrators. What forces for change, also known as driving forces, exist? Increased demands for parental involvement, an increasingly complex educational situation, and changes in state legislation are among the forces that might have spurred the change.

Changes in the organization's environment, such as new laws or regulations, rapidly increasing competition, or an unpredictable rate of inflation, may require the organization to implement new structures or reward systems. New programs resulting from the availability of improved technology; changes in competition in education; or unusual requirements of the new generation of students, such as inclusion or mainstreaming, may also affect the institution.

Finally, reduced productivity and effectiveness, product quality, satisfaction, commitment, or increased turnover or absenteeism may

FIGURE 4.1 / Identifying Target Forces

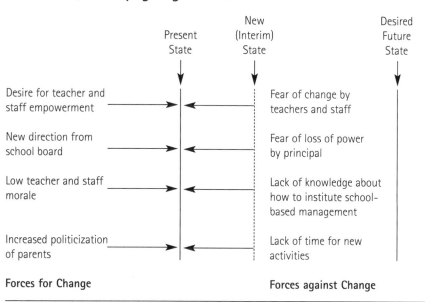

| | Present State | New (Interim) State | | Desired Future State |

Desire for teacher and staff empowerment → ← Fear of change by teachers and staff

New direction from school board → ← Fear of loss of power by principal

Low teacher and staff morale → ← Lack of knowledge about how to institute school-based management

Increased politicization of parents → ← Lack of time for new activities

Forces for Change   **Forces against Change**

call for changes in intra- or interdepartmental relations. One or two specific events external to the institution frequently precipitate the change. For example, the publication of *A Nation at Risk* in the 1980s caused a flurry of educational reforms that continue to this day.

Forces known as *resistance forces*, counteract the forces for change. Administrators might resist changes to their routines and supervisory activities; they may also be unwilling to relinquish their decision-making authority. Superintendents may be unwilling to allocate the resources required to change the culture. Identifying and then reducing resistance forces may be essential to making an individual or group receptive to change. The typical sources of resistance to change are illustrated in figure 4.2.

Forces against a change often reside within the institution and stem from rigid organizational structures and individual thinking. Specific forces against change include employees' distrust of the

FIGURE 4.2 / Sources of Resistance to Change

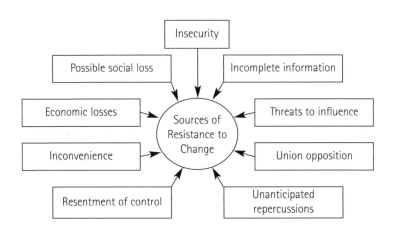

change agent, fear of change, desire to maintain power, and complacency; lack of resources to support the change; conflicts between individual and organizational goals; and organizational inertia against changing the status quo. These forces frequently combine into significant resistance to change.

Resistance results from a variety of factors. First, it occurs when a change ignores the needs, attitudes, and beliefs of an organization's members. If teachers, for example, have high security needs, they may see as threatening the increased attention to distance learning. Second, individuals resist change when they lack specific information about the change; they may not know when, how, or why it is occurring. Third, individuals may not perceive a need for change; they may feel that their organization is operating effectively and efficiently. In these cases change often is neither voluntary nor requested by organization members. Fourth, organization members frequently have a we–they mentality that causes them to view the change agent as their enemy, particularly when change is imposed by representatives outside of the immediate work site. Fifth, members may view change as a threat to the prestige and security of the institution. They may perceive the change in procedures or policies as a commentary that their performance is inadequate. Sixth, employees may perceive the change as a threat to their expertise, status, or security. Introduction of a new computer-aided instructional system, for example, may cause teachers to feel that they lack sufficient knowledge to perform their jobs; revision of an organization's structure may challenge their relative status in the organization, as our example of site-based management might do; introduction of a new reward system may threaten their feelings of job security. For effective change to occur, the change agent must confront each of these factors and overcome the resulting resistance. It helps a great deal if the change agent has engendered a sense of mutual trust and respect among his or her colleagues before the effort to effect change begins. Table 4.1 illustrates an example of a force field analysis. Table 4.2 depicts an action plan derived from the forces identified in Table 4.1.

Building an Action Plan

Following identification of the forces for and against change, the change agent must identify alternative actions for changing each force, and then organize them into an action plan. The analytical approach described here must be supplemented with a consideration of individuals' psychological reactions to change, and the development of appropriate strategies for dealing with them. It can also use action research methodology as a basis of studying and intervening in organizational situations. In action research, the change agent collaborates extensively with the entire school community in gathering and feeding back data. Together they collect and discuss the data, and then use the data for planning.[14]

Consider the possible reluctance of the principal to reduce her involvement in decision making, a force against a site-based management at the Washington School. The following actions could reduce this reluctance: implementing the change slowly, educating the prin-

TABLE 4.1 / Example of a Force Field Analysis

Problem: The pupils in Hughes Middle School are not developing good reading skills.

Facilitating Forces (+)	Restraining Forces (−)
Instructional Materials Center	Student transiency (over district average)
Full-time librarian	Bilingual population
Budgeted for 3 aides	Bimodal distribution of teachers (many
Funded ESL program	first year)
New reading series	New reading series program; no inservice
Assistant principal is a reading specialist	Parental involvement in school activities
State-mandated and -funded tutorial	slight
program	Little study room in homes—high number
Most children walk to school (no bus	of apartment and project dwellers
students)	Teacher turnover above district average
Expressed teacher concerns	Single-parent and two-wage-earner
Flexible schedule	homes (people not readily available)
	No role models
	Staff overload

cipal about the value of the change, or testing an experimental version of the new procedures to increase teacher and staff participation. Another intervention would be to identify a school where site-based management has been successful and have the principal visit that school. This is called the *best practices* approach. An example of an analysis of target forces affecting change at the Washington School is illustrated in table 4.3 on page 52.

Overcoming resistance to change is a daily issue for administrators or external change agents. Employees can sabotage change efforts and, ultimately, decrease their effectiveness. Resistance to change can result in lowered productivity, increased absenteeism, and decreased motivation. In the extreme, it can lead to work stoppages. The change agent must plan ways to overcome resistance to change, such as that depicted in figure 4.2.

The individual(s) responsible for the change should maintain open and frequent communication with the individuals, groups, or organi-

TABLE 4.2 / Action Planning: The Problem Resolution Document

Project: Improving the reading skills of seventh- and eighth-grade students at Hughes
Middle School

Project Manager: Kay Weise, Assistant Principal
Completion Date: June 1*
Start Date: August 15

Actions	Start/Complete	Relation to Force Field (What +/−)	Coordinator
Volunteers Program	10/1 cont.	#5(−)	Holland
After-school study program	11/1 cont.	#6(−)	Norris
"Why I Read" speakers	11/1–6/1	#9(−)	Carspecken
New teacher inservice program:	8/15–2/15	#6(+)	Craig
Reading in subject areas		#9(+)	
		#3(−)	
Reader of the Month Award	9/15–6/1	#1(+)	Tanner
		#2(+)	
"Here's an Author"	2/1–3/1	#9(−)	Strahan
Storytelling Time	10/5–5/15	#2(+)	Miller
		#3(+)	
		#10(+)	

*Actions #1 and #2 continue beyond June.

zations involved; for example, he or she might schedule regular informational meetings for all employees affected by the change. The change agent also should consider the needs of individual employees because responding to needs helps to develop in individuals a vested interest in and, ultimately, support for the change. Finally, where possible, the change agent should encourage voluntary change. Establishing a climate of innovation and experimentation can reduce the organization's tendency to maintain the status quo.

Development of an action plan concludes with a specification of each action in the order it will be performed. You can continue the analysis for the Washington School, or try a similar analysis with an organizational change situation you have faced. Be sure to perform all of the steps described above. Exhibit 4.1 on page 53 summarizes these steps.

TABLE 4.3 / An Example of an Analysis of Target Forces at the Washington School

Target Forces	Alternate Actions	Feasibility	Action Priority
Fear of change by the principal, teachers, and staff	Implement change slowly	Moderate; change can occur over a 12-month period	High
	Educate staff about the change	High; easy and relatively low cost	High
	Illustrate the benefits of the new system	High; easy and relatively low cost	High
	Pilot-test the system for small group	Moderate; time-consuming and pilot may be difficult to design	Medium-high
	Involve staff in planning the change	High; time-consuming but important to acceptance	Medium
Lack of knowledge about how to institute new programs	Offer training in culture change	High; important to eventual implementation	High
	Provide new policies and procedures	High; important to system implementation	Medium

A Case in Point

Suppose you were the principal of a middle school with an enrollment of 800 students. The school's student body is racially and culturally heterogeneous, but the majority of the students are from low-income families. You have recently become aware that the reading program in the school is suspect in light of declining standardized test results. Seventh- and eighth-grade students are not doing as well as might be expected.

In addition to declining standardized test scores (compared with local and national norms), the reading teachers report that there seems to be a declining interest in reading, and the librarian reports that book circu-

---

EXHIBIT 4.1 / Summary of Steps in Change

1. Identify forces for change.
2. Identify forces against change.
3. Brainstorm actions to reduce forces against change.
4. Brainstorm actions to enhance forces for change.
5. Assess feasibility of each action specified.
6. Prioritize actions.
7. Build an action plan from ranking of actions.
8. Develop timetable and budget for action plan.

---

lation has decreased in the last year or so. Your senior high school counterparts have expressed concern that your students do not seem as well-prepared upon entrance to high school as they have been in the past.

You conclude from this evidence that the reading program is in need of review. Thus, you engage in a force field analysis to determine the forces in favor and opposed to such a change. An example of a partial force field analysis on this problem appears in table 4.4.

Once the force field analysis has been completed, it is time to generate ideas for interventions that will ameliorate the problem. Creative thought is imperative, and one way of generating it is to engage in brainstorming, or Nominal group or Delphi techniques. Figure 2.1 show results of interventions that these techniques could generate.

■ **A CASE STUDY**

The assessment of favorable and opposing forces regarding the ILA program involved an individual and a group assessment. For example, certain groups were expected to oppose any change that would be perceived as altering the character of the educational program. The senior teachers were such a group. Interventions were formulated to deal with these groups. For example, the proposal began as a whole language program, but was altered to an integrated program to allay the fears of these teachers.

The original ILA proposal was revised further to accommodate the legitimate needs and preferences of various groups. The distinctive features of

TABLE 4.4 / Approaches to Dealing with Resistance to Change

Approach	Commonly Used in Situations	Advantages	Drawbacks
Education and communication	Where there is a lack of information or inaccurate information and analysis	Once persuaded, people will often help with the implementation of change	Can be very time-consuming if lots of people are involved
Participation and involvement	Where the initiators do not have all the information they need to design the change and where others have considerable power to resist	People who participate will be committed to implementing change	Can be very time-consuming if participators design an inappropriate change
Facilitation and support	Where people are resisting because of adjustment problems	No other approach works as well with adjustment problem.	Can be time-consuming and still fail
Negotiation and agreement	Where someone or some group will clearly lose out in a change and where that group has considerable power to resist	Sometimes it is a relatively easy way to avoid major resistance	Can be too expensive in many cases if it alerts others to negotiate for compliance
Manipulation and cooptation	Where other tactics will not work or are too expensive	It can be a relatively quick and inexpensive solution to resistance problems	Can lead to future problems if people feel manipulated
Explicit and implicit coercion	Where speed is essential, and the change initiators possess considerable power	It is speedy and can overcome any kind of resistance	Can be risky if it leaves people mad at the initiators

the program were determined as a means to accommodate various pressure groups in the school community. Initiation of the program at pilot schools was adopted, for example, to satisfy the faculty who felt that the infrastructure to support a new curriculum program was not yet present in the school system.

The inclusion of whole language-related concepts, such as mapping and metacognition through journal writing in other subject areas, allowed us to engender the support of the faculty because it offered the opportunity for those other than reading and language arts teachers to own the program, as well.

In addition to group considerations, those individuals who supported or opposed the ILA program were identified. We systematically listed each member of the faculty and staff and tried to determine where he or she would stand on the issue. After appropriate interventions were identified for each individual, committee members who had a relationship with the person in question were assigned to implement them. We had innumerable luncheon meetings with various individuals who opposed the program and made certain that the meetings included at least one colleague with whom these individuals were friendly, or for whom they had great respect. Care must be taken during this phase, however, that the change agent(s) does not ignore those who are in favor of the change. Their support must not be taken for granted. They should be affirmed and used to neutralize the opposing forces.

Another method of neutralizing the opposing forces and reinforcing the favorable ones is to prepare answers to the most commonly raised questions. The change agent(s) anticipates the questions that may be raised and answers them proactively. This approach sometimes can neutralize an opposing individual or group before the individual or group has a chance to mobilize around a certain issue.

While assessing opposing and favorable forces, the change agent(s) should be considering the next step in the integrated change process: selecting the best alternative. As pointed out in discussing assessment of forces, the best alternative most likely will be affected by the concessions that often need to be made to garner support for the change or reform.

Diagnostic Checklist

Here are a few questions you can address in your institution's assessment of forces:

1. Is a *force field analysis* being performed?
2. Is it adequately identifying *favorable and opposing forces*?
3. Is there a systematic plan to *affirm and strengthen* the favorable forces?
4. Is there a systematic plan to *neutralize* the opposing forces?

Endnotes

1. E. Mark Hanson, *Educational Administration and Organizational Behavior* (Boston: Allyn and Bacon, 1991), p. 353.

2. Richard Carlson, "Barriers to Change in Public Schools," in *Change Processer in Public Schools*, Richard Carlson et al., eds. (Eugene: University of Oregon, Center for the Advanced Study of Educational Administration, 1965).

3. Thomas Timar and David Kirp, *Managing Educational Excellence* (New York: Falmer, 1988), pp. 85-95.

4. Goodwin Watson, "Resistance to Change," in *The Planning of Change*, Warren Bennis et al., eds. (New York: Holt, Rinehart and Winston, 1969), p. 488.

5. Ibid., p. 351.

6. William Savage, *Interpersonal and Group Relations in Educational Administration* (Glenview, IL: Scott, Foresman, 1968), p. 190.

7. James G. March and Herbert A. Simon, *Organizations* (New York: John Wiley & Sons, 1958).

8. Edgar Huse, *Organizational Development and Change* (New York: West, 1975), pp. 112-13.

9. Watson, "Resistance to Change," pp. 487-96.

10. F. J. Roethlisberger and W. J. Dickson, *Management and the Worker* (Cambridge: Harvard University Press, 1938).

11. Neal Gross, Joseph Giacquinta, and Marilyn Bernstein, *Implementing Organizational Innovations* (New York: Basic Books, 1971).

12. Louis Smith and Pat Keith, *Anatomy of Educational Innovation: An Organizational Analysis of an Elementary School* (New York: John Wiley & Sons, 1971).

13. Albert Shanker, "Reforming the Reform Movement," *Educational Administration Quarterly* 24 (1988): 370.

14. W. French, Organization development—Objectives, assumptions, and strategies, *California Management Review* 12 (1969): 23-34.

5

Selecting Alternatives

There is no way to make people like change.
You can make them feel less threatened by it.
— Frederick O'R. Hayes

While the already mentioned steps in the integrated change process are being addressed, the change agent should establish a committee of "believers" to begin considering the best alternative available to effect the proposed reform. Ideally, a deliberative consideration of the various alternatives should be undertaken, and the most cost-efficient and effective alternative should be chosen. All too often, however, the powers that be have chosen the alternative already and the change agent is expected simply to implement it. In our example regarding site-based management, the reform was chosen by fiat. At the very least, the change agent should be free to adapt the reform to meet local needs.

Another phenomenon that sometimes occurs during this phase of the change process is the tendency to *satisfice*, or choose the alternative that offends the fewest individuals and/or groups, rather than choosing the best alternative. As described in the discussion of the ILA case study in chapter 4, the reform often is revised so that it satisfies opposing groups, rather than because it is the best possible alternative.

Satisficing is a term coined by Herbert Simon, a Nobel Prize winner in economics, who was critical of the so-called rational model of decision making, which indicates that decision makers develop and analyze all of the possible alternatives and select the best one available. According to Simon, however, it is at this point in the decision-making process where, rather than the best possible alternative being chosen, in the interest of efficiency the decision maker will *satisfice*, or sacrifice the optimal for a solution or alternative that is satisfactory or good enough. For example, if a school is trying to decide between the traditional phonetic approach versus the whole language approach to teaching reading, the change agent(s) may satisfice and choose an integrated model that combines the best aspects of both the phonetic and whole language approaches. Thus, the change agent(s) may sacrifice the optimal solution for one that satisfies the greatest number of constituencies.[1]

In a similar approach to selecting an alternative, the model known as *decision making by objection* prompts decision makers not to seek an optimal solution to a problem, but to choose a course of action that does not have a high probability of making matters worse.[2] The decision makers first produce a rough description of an acceptable resolution of the situation. Then they propose a course of action, accompanied by a description of the positive outcomes of the action. Objections to the action are raised, further delimiting the problem and defining an acceptable resolution. The decision makers repeat this process, creating a series of courses of action, each one having fewer objections than the previous one. Finally, the most acceptable alternative evolves.

The Garbage Can Model

As mentioned earlier, another model of selecting alternatives that emphasizes the unsystematic quality of much decision making in educational institutions is the *garbage can model*.[3] In an institution with unclear goals, uncertain means of achieving the goals, and changing participants in decision making, a diverse set of problems and solutions are presented simultaneously. The decision maker or change agent should recognize that serendipitous decisions may occur. Sometimes decisions fit solutions to problems in a way that resolves the problem, removing both the problem and solution from further consideration. The researchers note that this matching often occurs somewhat at random, and use the image of participants dumping problems and solutions into a "garbage can" to reflect how problems and solutions may be mixed together. If solutions and problems meet at the right time to make a choice, a rational outcome or choice is made; otherwise no decision results. For example, suppose a school district has been declining in enrollment because of an aging neighborhood. One of the alternatives may be to close some schools. However, if a farmer decides to sell some land, and a developer purchases it to build new homes, an alternative serendipitously presents itself that precludes having to take the less desirable alternative of closing schools.

More recent expansions of this model try to make the decision maker a more explicit part of the action by citing him or her as able to take advantage of opportunities when problems and solutions match.

Generating Alternatives

Once the force field analysis described in chapter 3 has been completed, it is time to generate alternatives that could be implemented to address the identified need effectively. Generally, a small committee representing as many of the school's constituencies as appropriate should be established. The members of the committee should be those who are advocates of change with possibly a naysayer or two to act as devil's advocates. In preparation for their work, committee members should be provided with the latest research findings regarding the reform being considered and be encouraged to make themselves aware of successful uses of the alternatives being considered. This *best prac-*

tices approach can be effective in identifying possible alternatives and convincing staff members of the reform's efficacy. The alternative that is finally chosen should be the one that best fits your local needs and should be selected according to its (a) rationale, (b) proven effectiveness, (c) resource requirements, (d) distinctive qualities, (e) mission appropriateness, and (f) cost/benefits.

Improving Alternative Selection

How can change agents overcome barriers, reduce biases, and make more effective decisions regarding the selection of the appropriate reform alternative? There are at least five techniques that can improve the alternative selection process: (a) brainstorming, (b) the nominal group technique, (c) the Delphi technique, (d) consensus mapping, and (e) creative thinking.

Brainstorming

Groups or individuals use brainstorming to generate many alternatives for consideration in the selection process. In brainstorming, the group lists as many alternatives as possible without evaluating the feasibility of any alternative. For example, if a cost reduction program is needed in a school district to offset continuing budget deficits, the change agent(s) might be charged with listing all of the ways of reducing costs in a school system. The absence of evaluation encourages group members to generate rather than defend ideas. Then, after ideas have been generated, they are evaluated, and selections are made. Although brainstorming can result in many shallow and useless ideas, it can also motivate members to offer new and innovative ideas. It works best when individuals have a common view of what constitutes a good idea, but it is more difficult to use when specialized knowledge or complex implementation is required. Since most educational reforms are complex in nature, brainstorming can only be used effectively in a limited number of cases and as part of the alternative generation process rather than as the essence of it.

Nominal Group Technique

The nominal group technique is a structured group meeting that helps resolve differences in group opinion by having individuals generate and then rank order a series of ideas in the problem-solving, alternative generation, or decision-making stage of a planning process.[4] A group of individuals is presented with a stated problem. Each person individually offers alternative solutions in writing. The group then shares the solutions and lists them on a chart, as in brainstorming. Group members discuss and clarify the ideas, then they rank and vote their preference for the various ideas. If the group has not reached an agreement, they repeat the ranking and voting procedure until the group reaches some agreement. Figure 5.1 illustrates the steps.

A more recent version of the nominal group technique emphasizes anonymity of input, pursuing a single purpose in any one group meeting, collecting and distributing inputs before a meeting, and delaying evaluation until all inputs are displayed. It also ensures opportunities for discussing displayed items before voting and limits discussion to pros and cons, allowing any individual to reword items, always using anonymous voting, and providing a second vote option.

The size of the group and the diverse expertise of its members increase the usefulness of the nominal group technique. It encourages each group member to think individually and offer ideas about the content of a proposal, and then directs group discussion. It moves the group toward problem resolution by systematically focusing on top-ranked ideas and eliminating less valued ones. The nominal group technique also encourages continued exploration of the issues, provides a forum for the expression of minority viewpoints, gives individuals some time to think about the issues before offering solutions, and provides a mechanism for reaching a decision expediently through the ranking-voting procedure. It fosters creativity by allowing extensive individual input into the process. Strong personality types

FIGURE 5.1 / Steps in Nominal Ranking

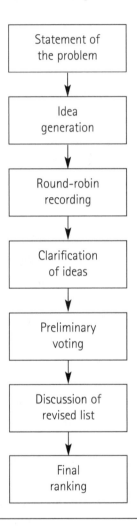

dominate the group less often because of the opportunity for systematic input by all group members. It encourages innovation, limits conflict, emphasizes equal participation by all members, helps generate consensus, and incorporates the preferences of individuals in decision-making choices. However, unless the change agent is trained in use of this technique and the ones that follow, it is more prudent to use an organizational consultant trained in these techniques to act as a facilitator.

The Delphi Technique

The Delphi technique structures group communication by dealing with a complex problem in four phases: (a) exploration of the subject by individuals, (b) reaching understanding of the group's view of the issues, (c) sharing and evaluating any reasons for differences, and (d) final evaluation of all information. In the conventional Delphi, as shown in figure 5.2, a small group designs a questionnaire, which is completed by a larger respondent group; the results are then tabulated and used in developing a revised questionnaire, which is again completed by the larger group. Thus, the results of the original polling are fed back to the respondent group to use in subsequent responses. This procedure is repeated until the issues are narrowed, responses are focused, or consensus is reached. In another format, a computer summarizes the results, thus replacing the small group. Such group decision support systems have increased the focus on the task or problem, the depth of analysis, communication about the task and clarifying information and conclusions, effort expended by the group, widespread participation of group members, and consensus reaching.[5]

Delphi is very helpful in a variety of circumstances. First, if the decision makers cannot apply precise analytical techniques to solving the problem, but prefer to use subjective judgments on a collective basis, Delphi can provide input from a large number of respondents. Second, if the individuals involved have failed to communicate effectively in the past, the Delphi procedures offer a systematic method for ensuring that their opinions are presented. Third, the Delphi does not require face-to-face interaction, so it succeeds when the group is too large for such a direct exchange. Fourth, when time and cost prevent frequent group meetings or when additional premeeting communi-

FIGURE 5.2 / Steps in the Delphi Technique

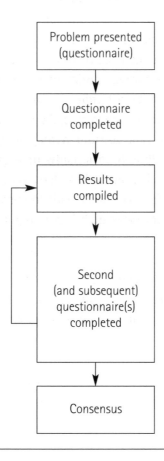

cation between group members increases the efficiency of the meeting held, the Delphi technique offers significant value for decision making. Fifth, the Delphi can overcome situations where individuals disagree strongly or where anonymity of views must be maintained to protect group members. Finally, the Delphi technique reduces the likelihood of groupthink; it prevents one or more members from dominating by their numbers or strength of their personality.

Consensus Mapping

Consensus mapping, which works best with multidimensional, complex problems that have interconnected elements and many sequential steps, begins after a steering committee has developed, clarified, and evaluated a list of ideas or alternatives. First, a person acting as facilitator encourages participants to search for clusters and categories of listed ideas and alternatives. This search for structure includes listing and discussing alternative clusters and categories by the entire group or subgroups and then production of a single classification scheme by group members working as a group, in pairs, or in trios.[6] Then the facilitator consolidates the different schemes developed by subgroups into a representative scheme that acts as a *straw man* map for the entire group. Group members next work to revise the straw man into a mutually acceptable solution. When there is more than one committee, or there are subcommittees, a representative from each presents its revised map to members of other subcommittees. Finally, representatives from each task group produce a single, consolidated map or solution.

Creative Thinking

Creativity in alternative selection is concerned with changing traditional patterns of thinking. Individuals try to restructure a pattern to reassemble it and view the problem differently. In popular parlance, they try to move out of their *paradigm*. Like brainstorming, which is a type of creative or lateral thinking, such thinking should focus on generation of alternatives, not on evaluation and selection. Suspending judgment about the correctness of an alternative facilitates creative thinking. Individuals can delay judgment about the relevance of information to the decision being considered, the validity of an idea for themselves or others, or the validity of an idea offered by another person. Delaying judgment encourages ideas to survive longer and spawns other ideas. It also motivates other people to offer ideas they normally would reject and stimulates new ideas, and it may result in the development of a new, more useful frame of reference for assessing them.

Individuals can use a variety of techniques to encourage their creative thinking. First, they can use alternative thinking languages, such as expressing a problem in mathematical rather than verbal terms or using visual models rather than verbal expressions of a problem. For example, participants might express alternatives graphically, in the form of a decision tree. Decision makers also can develop a questioning attitude as a way of gaining additional information. They also might make lists as a way of increasing their ability to process the information gained. Creative decision makers repeatedly challenge their assumption—for example, they may ask why repeatedly about information gathered and alternatives considered. Or other individuals or group members might take a devil's advocate approach to evaluating alternatives and choosing a final solution to a problem. Educators have a head start in assuming this role, because they have been trained to be critical thinkers. Creating analogies, reversing situations, and breaking alternatives into their component parts also fosters more creative decision making.

Top-Down and Bottom-Up Strategies

We often hear about the alleged virtues of bottom-up versus top-down strategies for generating educational reforms. The minority view is that top-down strategies are more effective. The fact of the matter is that neither of these strategies is maximally effective in isolation. Rather, coordinating top-down and bottom-up strategies for educational reform is most effective.

Small- and large-scale studies of top-down strategies have demonstrated consistently that local implementation fails in the vast majority of cases. The best known study of voluntary adoption of top-down movements is the Rand Change Agent study conducted by Berman and McLaughlin and associates.[7] They investigated federally sponsored educational programs adopted in 293 sites and found that, even though adoption was voluntary, districts often took on change projects for opportunistic rather than substantial reasons.

On a more sweeping scale, Sarason argues that billions of dollars have been spent on top-down reforms with little to show for it. Sarason observes that such reform efforts do have an implicit theory of change: Change can come about by proclaiming new policies, or by legislation, or by new performance standards, or by creating a shape-up-or-ship-out ambiance, or all of the preceding. It is a conception that in principle is similar to how you go about creating and improving an assembly line—that is, what it means to those who work on the assembly line is of secondary significance, if it has any significance at all. The workers will change.[8]

In short, centralized reform mandates have a poor track record as instruments for educational improvement. This failure has led some to conclude that only decentralized, locally driven reform can succeed. Site-based management is currently the most prominent manifestation of this focus. So far, however, the claim of superiority of grassroots initiatives is primarily theoretical. In reviewing evidence on site-based management in *The New Meaning of Educational Change*,[9] one can conclude that restructuring reforms that involved decision making by schools may have altered governance procedures, but they do not affect the teaching–learning process in any significant way.

The evidence that bottom-up strategies are no more effective than top-down ones continues to mount. Taylor and Teddlie[10] draw similar conclusions in their study of the extent of classroom change in "a district widely acclaimed as a model of restructuring." They examined classrooms in thirty-three schools (sixteen from pilot schools that had established site-based management programs and seventeen from nonpilot schools in the same district). They did find that teachers in the pilot schools reported higher levels of participation in decision making, but they found no differences in teaching strategies (teacher-directed instruction and low student involvement dominated in both sets of cases). Further, there was little evidence of teacher-teacher collaboration. Extensive collaboration was reported in only two of the thirty-three schools, and both were nonpilot schools. Taylor and Teddlies observe: "Teachers in this study did not alter their practice . . . Increasing their participation in decision making did not overcome norms of autonomy so that teachers would feel empowered to collaborate with their colleagues." In sum, then, decentralized initiatives do not fare any better than centralized reforms.

A number of educational researchers[11] have concluded that organizations, including schools, that underwent successful revitalization followed a particular sequence in which individual, small-group, and informal behavior began to change first (bottom-up, if you will), which in turn was reinforced and further propelled by changes in formal design and procedures (structures, personnel practices, compensation systems, etc.) in the organization (top-down). Both local and central levels can be active and influential at all phases. These studies and my own experience have led me to promote an integrated change process that involves both top-down and bottom-up strategies that operate simultaneously in effectively implemented reform.

Top-down strategies result in conflict, or superficial compliance, or both. Expecting local units to flourish through laissez-faire decentralization leads to drift, narrowness, or inertia. Combined strategies that capitalize on the central office's strengths (to provide direction, incentives, networking, and monitoring) and the local school's capacities (to learn, create, respond, and contribute) are more likely to achieve greater overall effectiveness. Such systems also have greater accountability, given that the need to obtain political support for ideas is built into their patterns of interaction.

Simultaneous top-down/bottom-up strategies are essential because dynamically complex societies are full of surprises. Only the negotiated capacity and strengths of the entire school community are capable of promoting school improvement while retaining the capacity to learn from new patterns, whether anticipated or not. Finally, one level cannot wait for the other level to act. Systems do not change by themselves; individuals and groups change systems. Breakthroughs occur when productive connections amass, creating growing pressure for systems to change. The more that top-down and bottom-up forces are coordinated, the more likely that complex systems will move toward greater effectiveness.

■ A CASE STUDY

Choosing the best alternative regarding the reading and language arts curriculum involved examining successful curricula in other school districts to identify the best fit for our school system. After extensive research, which included brainstorming, nominal group, and Delphi technique activities, we settled on an integrated model that included the best aspects of the whole language approach and the traditional phonics approach.

Our next step in the alternative selection process was to review the existing integrated language arts programs in the nation and model our program after the one that best met our local needs, the *best practices* approach to selecting an alternative. We looked at what programs (a) best fit our school system's mission, (b) were proven effective, (c) were cost effective, and (d) had distinctive qualities. We narrowed the search to those programs used in the Milwaukee and Johnson City, New York, school districts. Using the Delphi technique, we settled on features from both programs. We augmented these programs with several distinctive features of our own and submitted the resulting proposal to the school community for review, analysis, and approval. What evolved was an ILA program that we decided to pilot at ten schools that were representative of the population of schools in the school district. If successful in the pilot schools, the program would be implemented systemwide.

Diagnostic Checklist

Here are a few questions you can address is assessing your institution's success in creating and selecting alternatives:

1. Is *creative thinking* being used in developing possible alternatives?
2. Are representatives of *all segments* of the school community involved in the selection process?

3. Does the alternative selected relate to *local* needs?
4. Are both *top-down and bottom-up* strategies being employed?

Endnotes

1. H. A. Simon, *The New Science of Management Decision* (New York: Harper, 1960).

2. P. A. Anderson, Decision making by objection and the Cuban Missile crisis, *Administrative Science Quarterly* 28 (1983): 201–22.

3. M. Masuch and P. LaPotin, Beyond garbage cans: An AI model of organizational choice, *Administrative Science Quarterly* 34 (1989): 38–67.

4. Robert H. Palestini, *The Ten-Minute Guide to Educational Leadership* (Lancaster: Technomic Publishing, 1998), p. 80.

5. Ibid., p. 85.

6. Ibid., p. 86.

7. Michael G. Fullan, Coordinating top-down and bottom-up strategies for educational reform, *The Governance of Curriculum Journal* 28 (1995): 30–48.

8. S. Sarason, *The Predictable Failure of Educational Reform* (San Francisco: Jossey-Bass 1990).

9. Ibid., 123.

10. D. Taylor and C. Teddlie, Restructuring and the classroom: A view from a reform district, paper presented at the Annual Meeting of the American Educational Research Association, San Francisco (1992).

11. Fullan, "Coordinating top-down and bottom-up strategies," p. 36.

6

Promoting Ownership

Change not the masses but change the fabric of your
own soul and your own vision and you change all.
— Vachel Lindsay

It is a truism in education, and in other fields, that if a change or
reform is to be implemented successfully, it must have the support of
the faculty and staff. Consequently, we often hear managers suggest
that a new program does not have a chance of succeeding unless the
employees take ownership of it. Most of us agree with the common
sense of this assertion. But how does a leader effectively promote employee ownership? Let me suggest four steps as a beginning:

- *Respect people.* As we have indicated earlier, this starts with ap-
  preciating the diverse gifts that individuals bring to your institution. The key is to dwell on the strengths of your coworkers,
  rather than on their weaknesses. This does not mean that disciplinary action or even dismissal will never become necessary.
  What it does mean, however, is that we should focus on the formative aspect of the employee evaluation process before we engage
  in the summative part. Leaders are obligated to develop colleague's
  skills and place them in situations that will maximize their potential for success.

- *Let belief guide policy and practice.* We spoke earlier of developing a culture of civility in your institution. If there is an environment of mutual respect and trust, the institution will flourish. Leaders need to let their belief or value system guide their behavior. Style is merely a consequence of what we believe and what is in our hearts.

- *Recognize the need for covenants.* Contractual agreements cover such things as salary, fringe benefits, and working conditions. They are part of organizational life, and there is a legitimate need for them. But in today's educational institutions, where the best people working in our schools are similar to volunteers, we need covenantal relationships.[1] Our best workers may choose their employers. They usually choose the institution where they work based on reasons less tangible than salaries and fringe benefits. They do not need contracts, they need covenants. Covenantal relationships enable educational institutions to be civil, hospitable, and understanding of individuals' differences and unique nature. They allow administrators to recognize that treating everyone equally is not necessarily treating everyone fairly. Sometimes exceptions need to made, and certain individuals need to be treated in special ways.

- *Understand that culture counts more than structure.* An educational institution recently went through a particularly traumatic time when the credibility of the administration was questioned by the faculty and staff. Various organizational consultants were interviewed to facilitate a healing process. Most of the consultants spoke of making the necessary structural changes to create a culture of trust. Finally, a consultant was hired whose attitude was that organizational structure has nothing to do with trust. Interpersonal relations based on mutual respect and an atmosphere of goodwill are what creates a culture of trust. Would you rather work as part of a school with an outstanding reputation or work as part of a group of outstanding individuals? Many times these two characteristics go together, but if one had to make a choice, most people likely would opt to work with outstanding individuals.

It Starts with Trust

These are exciting times in education. Revolutionary steps are being taken to restructure schools and rethink the teaching–learning process. Empowerment, total quality management, the use of technology, and strategic planning are becoming the norm. However, while these reforms have the potential to influence education in significantly positive ways, they must be based on a strong foundation to achieve their full potential.

Achieving educational effectiveness is an incremental, sequential improvement process. This process begins by building a sense of security within each individual so that he or she can be flexible in adapting to changes within education. Addressing only skills or techniques, such as communication, motivation, negotiation, or empowerment, is ineffective when individuals in an organization do not trust its systems, themselves, or each other. An institution's resources are wasted when invested only in training programs that assist administrators in mastering quick-fix techniques that at best attempt to manipulate and at worst reinforce mistrust.

The challenge is to transform relationships based on insecurity, adversarialism, and politics to those based on mutual trust. Trust is the beginning of effectiveness and forms the foundation of a principle-centered learning environment that emphasizes strengths and devises innovative methods to minimize weaknesses. The transformation process requires an internal locus of control that emphasizes individual responsibility and accountability for change and for promoting effectiveness.

Effective Decisions

If one is expected to engender employee ownership of the change or reform, the change agent needs to be seen as making effective decisions. There are two important components of an effective decision, its quality and its acceptance.[2] A good-quality decision brings about the desired result while meeting relevant criteria and constraints. In our site-based management example, a good-quality decision would be to empower the staff with budget authority. Certainly a decision that transfers some authority from the administration to those closest to the students would be a good-quality one in this instance. Also, a decision that meets the needs of those affected by the decision, including students, faculty, staff, administrators, and taxpayers, would qualify. So too would a decision that meets the financial, human, time, and other constraints existing in the situation.

The quality of the decision depends in part on the level of the decision maker's technical or task skills, interpersonal or leadership skills, and decision-making skills. Technical or task skills refers to the individual's knowledge of the particular area in which the decision is being made. In the decisions that must be made regarding site-based management, task skills refers to a knowledge of the costs involved; projected revenues, if any; educational product information; and school system overhead costs. Interpersonal or leadership skills relate to the way individuals lead, communicate with, motivate, and influence others. The principal of Washington School, for example, must be able to get the other stakeholders in the school system to accept the decision for which she is responsible. Effective communication should facilitate understanding and acceptance of the decision. Decision-making skills are the basic ability to perform the components of the decision-making process, including situational analysis; objective setting; and generation, evaluation, and selection of alternatives, as has been discussed.

The principal of the Washington School and any advisor she involves in the decision making must produce a decision that they and the rest of the school community can accept, one that they are willing to live with. For example, giving budgeting authority to the teachers might be a high-quality decision, but if the school board or the superintendent does not support it, there is not much chance of its being effective. Thus, acceptance of the decision is a characteristic that needs to be considered along with the quality of the decision.

The Vroom/Yetton Decision-Making Model

The administrative and organizational theory literature is in agreement about the two most important factors to be considered in determining the decision style that will produce the most effective decisions. While Vroom and Yetton's model includes the additional dimension of shared goals and conflict possibility, the two key elements are the quality and the acceptance of the decision, as described above. Figure 6.1 summarizes identification of the decision style that is most appropriate for particular problem types.[3]

The two key elements are quality, or the likelihood of one decision being more rational than another, and acceptance, or the extent to which acceptance or commitment on the part of subordinates is crucial to effective implementation of the decision. For example, if a new law is passed regarding education, and the administrator has to include it in the revised edition of the student handbook, the quality of the decision is more important than its acceptance. Therefore, the appropriate decision style is command. On the other hand, if acceptance is more important than quality, as in the development of a new teacher evaluation instrument, the proper decision style is consensus.

If both the quality and acceptance are of equal importance, such as whether to adopt a whole language approach to reading, consultation or group decision making is the appropriate style. Finally, if neither quality nor the acceptance is important, such as deciding what color to paint the school lockers, convenience is the applicable style.

Ethical Decision Making

In addition to evaluating the quality and acceptance of a decision, one can assess how well it meets the criterion of ethical fairness and justice. Consider, for example, a disastrous decrease in standardized test scores in a high school. Top administrators are faced with the decision of whether to risk public outrage and the possible transfer of significant numbers of students or gloss over the situation.

Administrators and staff can assess whether the decisions they

FIGURE 6.1 / The Dimensions of Effective Decisions

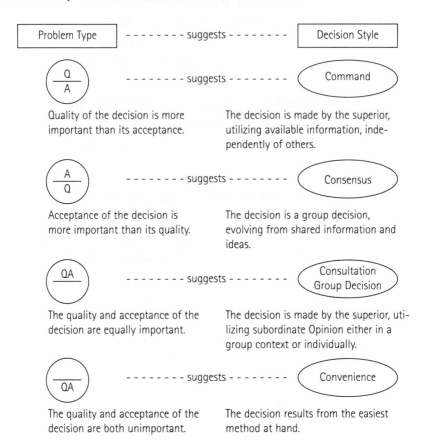

| Problem Type | - - - - - - - suggests - - - - - - - | Decision Style |

$\frac{Q}{A}$ - - - - - - - suggests - - - - - - - Command

Quality of the decision is more important than its acceptance.

The decision is made by the superior, utilizing available information, independently of others.

$\frac{A}{Q}$ - - - - - - - suggests - - - - - - - Consensus

Acceptance of the decision is more important than its quality.

The decision is a group decision, evolving from shared information and ideas.

$\frac{QA}{}$ - - - - - - - suggests - - - - - - - Consultation Group Decision

The quality and acceptance of the decision are equally important.

The decision is made by the superior, utilizing subordinate Opinion either in a group context or individually.

$\frac{}{QA}$ - - - - - - - suggests - - - - - - - Convenience

The quality and acceptance of the decision are both unimportant.

The decision results from the easiest method at hand.

The administrative and organizational theory literature (Maier 1962; Bridges, 1967; Vroom and Yetton, 1973) are in total agreement about the two most important factors to be considered in determining the decision style that will produce the most effective decisions. While Vroom and Yetton's model adds the dimension of shared goals and conflict possibility, the two key elements are also stressed: QUALITY and ACCEPTANCE. The diagram summarizes Maier's work in identifying the decision style that is most appropriate for particular problem types. The two key elements are defined as:

(1) Quality (Q)   The importance of quality—i.e., one solution is likely to be more rational than another. The extent to which the leader possesses sufficient information/expertise to make high-quality decisions by him or herself.

(2) Acceptance (A) The extent to which acceptance or commitment on the part of subordinates is crucial to effective implementation of the decision.

make are ethical by applying personal moral codes or society's codes of values; they can apply philosophical views of ethical behavior; or they can assess the potential harmful consequences of behaviors to certain constituencies. One way of thinking about ethical decision making suggests that a person who makes a moral decision first, must recognize the moral issue of whether a person's actions can hurt or help others; second, make a moral judgment; third, decide to attach greater priority to moral concerns than financial or other concerns, or establish their moral intent; and, finally, act on the moral concerns of the situation by engaging in moral behavior.[4] In making an ethical decision change agents can use the checklist in figure 6.2. In conclusion, therefore, by combining the components of effective decision making with the characteristics of an ethical decision, the change agent can accomplish two important points: increase employee ownership of change, and build a culture of trust and respect.

Empowerment

Empowerment is currently a topical issue and deserves to be. Empowering employees can have a motivating and energizing effect on their performance. Ironically, in the first wave of educational reforms in the 1980s teachers were identified as the problem. More recently, however, they have been identified as the solution. Critics of the early reforms argued that increasing state-mandated educational standards and the prescribed content and form of schooling were too rigid to produce learners who can think critically, synthesize, and create new information.

The 1990s saw reform reports that brought a new focus to the challenges of improving American education. A bottom-up approach to reform was common among the most influential of these reports, which were produced by The Holmes Group, The Carnegie Forum, and National Governors' Association.[5]

The reports stressed that teachers have been assigned one of society's most difficult tasks but have not been given the authority to resolve them. Effective teaching and learning consist of a complex mix

---

FIGURE 6.2 / General Ethical Checklist

	Yes	No
1. "Does my decision treat me, or my company, as an exception to a convention that I must trust others to follow?"	—	—
2. "Would I repel customers by telling them?"	—	—
3. "Would I repel qualified job applicants by telling them?"	—	—
4. "Have I been cliquish?	—	—
(If "Yes," answer questions 4a through 4c. If "No," skip to question 5.)		
4a. "Is my decision partial?"	—	—
4b. "Does it divide the constituencies of the company?"	—	—
4c. "Will I have to pull rank (use coercion) to enact it?"	—	—
5. "Would I prefer to avoid the consequences of this decision?"	—	—
6. "Did I avoid any of the questions by telling myself that I could get away with it?"	—	—

Reprinted with permission by JAI Press Inc., from M. R. Hyman, R. Skipper, and R. Tansey. Ethical codes are not enough, *Business Horizons* (March–April 1990), p. 17.

---

of intellect, spontaneity, insight, personal understanding, love, and patience. Rules, especially those imposed from afar, constrain the learning process rather than release it. The second wave of reform reports differed from the first by arguing that the restructuring should "empower teachers rather than manage them."[6]

According to Thomas Sergiovanni and John Moore,[7] empowerment is not the same as acknowledging the de facto discretion that already exists in the classroom. It is a deliberate effort to provide principals and teachers with the room, right, responsibility, and resources to make sensible decisions and informed professional judgments that reflect their circumstances.

The effort calls for enhancing the professional status of teachers by providing them with more autonomy, training, trust, and collegial opportunities to carry out their tasks—that is, not to treat teachers like factory workers who are told what to do, how to do it, and when to do it. The effectiveness of this task-oriented approach is also being questioned in industry, by the way. The concept of empowerment has become a force in education, not only with teachers, but also with other educational personnel. Our example of site-based management at the Washington School has empowerment as its basis. Every school should be given the freedom and flexibility to respond creatively to its educational objectives and, above all, to meet the needs of students. This approach engenders employee ownership and helps bring about change more effectively.

■ A CASE STUDY

In a change that is as complex as the inauguration of a new reading and language arts program, quality and acceptance of the change are important. Therefore, we needed to be certain that the program has high academic integrity to satisfy the quality issue, and has significant faculty and staff input to satisfy the acceptance issue. Thus, academic quality and employee ownership are both important if the ILA program is to navigate the school system approval process successfully.

As a result of these sensitivities, the change agents responsible for the ILA program did a number of things to ensure the quality and acceptance of the program. First, a task force, with members representing the entire school community, was commissioned. Its charge was to address the stagnation of the reading and language arts standardized test scores. When both the quality and the acceptance of a decision is important, Vroom and Yetton tell us that a collaborative approach to decision making should be taken. Thus, the task force engaged in collaborative type activities.

As mentioned earlier, the task force conducted a needs assessment to determine whether the school community perceived the same need as the superintendent and the school board. During the needs assessment process the school community was asked for possible solutions. In this way, many of those responding felt an integral part of the decision-making process. In addition to the needs assessment, the task force engaged an organizational development consultant to conduct focus groups to obtain further input on the matter. Finally, after the task force identified a number of alternatives to address the language arts issue, the Delphi technique was used to generate further alternatives and develop a survey to hone in on the preferred ones. The outcome of all of this collaboration was an integrated language arts program that was to be implemented on a pilot basis and, if effective, on a systemwide basis.

In the aggregate, the above components of the program fostered the employee ownership that is so important for successful implementation. Finally, after about a year of debate on this issue, we convinced the school community that the time for discernment and critical thinking was drawing to a close, and that it was now time to set aside our differences and join together as a community in support of this important endeavor. Because a culture of trust and respect had been established, and because we had a quality program that was accepted, the ILA program was accepted and approved overwhelmingly. None of this would have happened, however, if we had not taken the time and effort to develop a sense of employee ownership.

Diagnostic Checklist

Here are a few questions you can address in assessing whether you have created a sense of employee ownership in your institution:

1. Are efforts made to establish a sense of *trust and respect*?
2. Are the aspects of *quality and acceptance* being considered in the decision-making process?
3. Is the appropriate *decision-making style* being used in a given situation?
4. Is a sense of employee *ownership* being established and fostered?

Endnotes

1. Max de Pree, *Leadership Is an Art* (New York: Dell Publishing, 1989).
2. Robert H. Palestini, *Educational Administration: Leading with Mind and Heart* (Lancaster: Technomic Publishing, 1998).
3. Ibid., p. 254.
4. Ibid., p. 255.
5. E. Mark Hanson, *Educational Administration and Organizational Behavior* (Boston: Allyn and Bacon, 1991), p. 382.
6. Ibid., p. 383.
7. Thomas J. Sergiovanni and John H. Moore, *Schooling for Tomorrow* (Boston: Allyn and Bacon, 1988).

7

Providing Staff Development

If you have knowledge, let others light their candles at it.
— Margaret Fuller

Very often staff development, an essential part of the change process, is neglected or overlooked completely. Many educational reforms have failed because of an enthusiastic but ill-advised leader who has tried to implement a change before engaging in staff development. Sometimes, even when staff development is provided, it has been ineffective. Negative responses to organized efforts in the name of staff development are the result of a history of poor experiences with activities that have taken place in the name of inservice training. However well-intended such activities may have been, too frequently they have not addressed the needs of the individual or the institution. Better approaches exist and are effective if they recognize the needs of the individual, the needs of the institution, the nature of adult learners, the time and effort required, and the importance of staff development to the ultimate success of any change or reform.

Human Resources Development
Staff development is a form of human resources development, a process that uses developmental practices to bring about higher quality, greater productivity, and more satisfaction among employees as

organization members. It is a function of both an individual's knowledge, skills, and attitudes and the policies, structure, and management practices that make up the system in which the employee works. In a school setting, the ultimate goal of human resource development is to produce the highest-quality instruction and service to the students.1

The most important resource in an institution is its staff. When the staff's thinking is congruent with organizational needs, and when the staff is well-trained, adaptive, and motivated, effective schools result. To achieve this goal requires attention to the various ways in which human potential can be realized and to the variety of needs that any particular person and group may have at any particular stage of development.

A Staff Development Model

The field of organizational development has been characterized recently by a renewed interest in the human dimension of the institution. The interest in Edwards Deming's work in *Total Quality Management* and his emphasis on training and cooperatively established goals, as well as the success of such publications as *The One Minute Manager, Megatrends*, and *In Search of Excellence*, has directed much attention to the human resources development focus that successful organizations maintain.

The staff development model that we propose is sensitive to four factors: (a) the distinct nature of adult learners, (b) the various learning styles of staff members, (c) the varying time requirements needed to effect learning, and (d) the appropriate development process required.

Adult learners are at a stage of cognitive development that can be distinguished from that of the adolescent. It has long been thought that the stages of cognitive development terminate in one's early twenties. On the contrary, relatively recent research indicates that cognitive development continues well into adulthood. Generally, we learn in different ways when we become adults. For example, because adults tend to have more experience than younger people, they tend to learn in more of a cognitive style rather than according to the behaviorist model. Thus, adults gain new knowledge by connecting it with former knowledge. Younger learners, however, tend to learn in a stimulus/response-type model. It is important, therefore, to structure staff development efforts in the constructivist or interactive model of learning. Cooperative learning techniques, discussion groups, case studies, and active learning exercises need to be incorporated into the staff development activities. Talking heads alone will not do.

The various learning styles of adult learners should also be taken into consideration in any staff development effort. Adapting one's teaching style to the various learning styles of the staff should be a priority. Thus, along with lecturing, which may appeal to some individuals on the staff, other more interactive approaches such as those suggested above should be used. By varying their presentations, the staff developers will be assured that they appeal to the various learning styles in their audiences.

Another important factor to be considered in constructing a staff development program is the amount of time that it takes various individuals to master a concept or skill. Research has indicated that even individuals with average intelligence can learn complex concepts if given time. Thus, we can all learn, but it takes some of us longer to learn a given piece of knowledge than it does others. Therefore, assessment activities need to be incorporated into staff development efforts. From time to time the acquisition of knowledge needs to be assessed so that more time can be allotted to those who need it. Mastery by all is the goal of staff development. This goal can be achieved only if the varying time requirements for learning are taken into consideration.

Keeping the above considerations in mind, the staff developer is now ready to apply the appropriate training for the change or reform that is to be implemented. Knowledge of how the reform can be implemented successfully must be obtained. Ordinarily, this is accomplished by observing an institution where the reform has been effective. Often, it is wise to bring someone in who has had success in bringing about a similar change. However, make certain that guest speakers incorporate the points made above into their presentation.

Implementing a Staff Development Plan

Assuring the quality of a school staff has always been a concern of educational administrators. However, with increasing frequency of educational reforms, it becomes more of a priority. Innovations such as competency testing, site-based management, cooperative learning, whole language approaches, and outcomes-based assessment have made a quality staff development plan indispensable.

Characteristic of such quality staff development programs is implementation of a model similar to that presented above. Such a program requires an organized array of organizational responses, including clinical supervision, peer evaluation, development of job assignments, diagnostic and remedial programs, and the systematic cooperative relationship with intermediate units and institutions of higher education.

Ordinarily, a staff development plan begins with a needs assessment. However, in the case of a mandated change in the form of an educational reform, the need has already been established. Thus, the content of the staff development has been determined. The first step in the process then becomes an assessment of the skill level of the staff as a whole and individually. If an effective staff evaluation process is in place, the readiness level of the staff for a particular change is ascertained rather easily.

Such an evaluation of the staff reveals the need for both group and individual training. If a whole language reading program is to be adopted by a school, for example, how much preexisting knowledge, in any, the staff has is important in determining the amount and type of staff development that should be offered. It is not uncommon, however, to find that although the staff as a whole has the knowledge and skills to implement a change, certain individuals do not.

Individual Development Plans

The individual development plan should include a self-assessment. Individual staff members review their professional qualifications, skills, and interests. A personal judgment is made about how these skills may be maximized in the organizational setting and how any skill or knowledge deficiency can be addressed. There should be a meeting comparing the individual's self-assessment with any outside assessment that might be available. The outcome of this meeting should be a specific plan to have the individual acquire the knowledge and skills necessary to be a part of effectively implementing the reform in question. The next step in the process may be to assign a mentor to the individual staff member.

Mentoring

Mentoring proposes a relationship between peers, but not peers of equal knowledge and skills. The term *mentor* is derived from Greek mythology. Mentor was a friend and counselor to Ulysses's son when Ulysses set off on his ten-year journey. The complex role consisted of protector, advisor, teacher, and father figure to the young boy. In today's settings, a formalized mentor program typically involves a relationship between a seasoned employee of some stature and a younger, inexperienced colleague. In the context of staff development, the focus of the relationship is on advanced skills development and acquiring a knowledge base to implement the proposed change effectively.

Obviously, productive relationships are not automatic. Administrators interested in developing a quality mentoring system need to consider such aspects as the careful matching of the individuals, a good initial orientation, and a feedback and monitoring system. If these aspects are attended to, a mentoring system can be instrumental in bringing about an intended change.

Implications for Leaders of Change

In summary, then, there are at least four implications to the change agent who wants an effective staff development plan.

The development needs of the staff as a group and the various individuals must be assessed accurately. Self-assessment can be a starting point, but the leader also must conduct an investigation, using clinical supervision observations in the classroom, student data, and internal and external data sources.

High standards of performance must be established and evaluated. Setting these goals in conjunction with the staff and with individuals has been found to be highly motivating. The success of management by objective (MBO) is based on developing mutual acceptable goals and objectives.

Human resources development plans require careful planning and a variety of approaches. Both group and individual development plans must focus on recognized needs and must be monitored regularly.

Positive reinforcement techniques need to be used consistently and continually. Such reinforcement can help bring about the desired behavior.[2]

■ A CASE STUDY

Now the real work begins. How do we ensure the change is implemented properly, and how do we maximize its chances of success? One important answer is through effective staff development.

To prepare for success in the ILA program, we engaged in a number of professional development activities. We sent key members of the faculty and staff to visit the schools after which our program was fashioned. In turn, we had faculty from these institutions visit our schools, make presentations, and offer suggestions about how we could implement our program effectively. We also had a local university schedule professional development classes in whole language and interactive instructional techniques over the summer and offered incentives for our teachers to attend. We followed these classes with sessions during the school year to be certain that all of the teachers had been exposed to these innovations. Finally, we made certain that our new hires had experience with interactive and cooperative learning techniques and had training at their teacher preparation institutions in whole language models of instruction. If they had not, we set up a mentoring program whereby a faculty member with such experience was assigned to an inexperienced faculty member. In these ways we used staff development as a means of maximizing our chances of succeeding.

We also had Joel Barker, a well-known futurist, give a motivational presentation to our faculty and staff members. We made certain that every segment of the school community was prepared properly for this reform. In addition to preparation of the faculty and staff described above, we had various presentations, workshops, and conferences for students, parents, the school board, education advocacy groups, business leaders, and local politicians. We even had our elementary school principals address local Kiwanis, and Lions clubs, and chambers of commerce. After all of this, we felt confident that the entire school community was prepared for the transformation that was about to begin.

Diagnostic Checklist

Here are a few questions you can address in assessing the effectiveness of the staff development plan at your institution:

1. Is a staff *assessment and appraisal plan* in effect at your institution?
2. Is it used to develop a *staff development plan*?
3. Are both *group and individual* development plans in effect?
4. Is a *mentoring* system in effect?
5. Is *staff development* part of the process of change at your institution?

Endnotes

1. Gerald C. Ubben and Larry W. Hughes, *The Principal* (Boston: Allyn and Bacon, 1996), p. 241.
2. Ibid., p. 264.

8

Operationalizing Change

Behold the turtle. He makes progress
only when he sticks his neck out.
— James Bryant Conant

Action follows identification of target forces for and against change, selection of and implementation of intervention strategies, and development of a staff development plan. It is at this point that we operationalize the change, or give form to our vision. Although careful
preparation for change increases the chances of success, it does not
guarantee effective action. Placing the plan in operation requires estab-
lishment of the organizational structure that will best suit the change,
and development of an assessment process to determine if the change is
remaining on course. Briefing sessions, special seminars, or other means
of information dissemination must permeate the change effort. Operationalizing the change must include procedures for keeping all participants informed about the change activities and their effects.

The use of a broad-based steering committee to oversee the change
may increase its likelihood of success. Such a group, composed of representatives of all areas of the institution, can advise on program
budget and organizational policies and priorities. It is helpful if the
same task force is active throughout the change process in that it
guarantees needed continuity.

FIGURE 8.1 / Steps in Managing Large-Scale Change

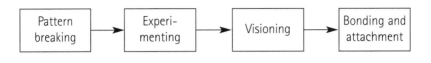

Further, the dynamic nature of organizational systems calls for flexibility in action. All efforts must include contingency plans for unanticipated cost, consequences, or resistance. A strong commitment to the change by top leaders can buffer change efforts from these difficulties and ensure the transfer of needed resources to the action plan.

Managing large-scale organizational change might require a more elaborate approach. The process includes at least four components: (a) pattern breaking, (b) experimenting, (c) visioning, and (d) bonding and attunement, as shown in figure 8.1.

Pattern breaking involves freeing the system from structures, processes, and functions that are no longer useful. An organization can be open to new options if it can relinquish approaches that no longer work, or experiences a *paradigm shift.* In the case of site-based management at the Washington School, replacing some of the structures and processes associated with the former nonschool-based management approach would be the first step toward operationalizing the change.

Experimenting by generating new patterns encourages flexibility and yields new options. Training small groups of administrators to institute teamwork illustrates this element. To experiment, organizations must have a philosophy and mechanisms in place that encourage innovation and creativity.

Visioning activities, such as building shared meaning throughout the institution and using the current mission statement, generate support for and commitment to the planned changes. Schoolwide meetings at the Washington School to share ideal views about site-based management would help accomplish this step.

In the last component, *bonding and attunement,* management attempts to integrate all facets of the institutional change to move members toward the new way of action by focusing them on important tasks and generating constructive interpersonal relationships.[1]

School Organization

To operationalize a reform properly, the change agent needs to be keenly aware of the existing culture and the structure of the institution, and what form of organizational structure will best facilitate successful implementation of the change. For ease of operation, the various schools of thought regarding organizational structure can be grouped into three types of organizational theory, namely, *classical organization theory, social systems theory,* and *open systems theory.*

Classical Organizational Theory

As figure 8.2 illustrates, all three bodies of theory are presented in contemporary management thinking, although they entered the mainstream at different times. The pioneer researchers did not originate the phenomena about which they wrote. When Max Weber began writing at the turn of the century about bureaucracy, elements of it had been present in descriptions of organized life back to ancient Rome and China.[2]

Most classical thinkers, such as Weber, Henri Fayol, and Frederick Taylor, lived through the Industrial Revolution as it went through its most fervent stages around the turn of the twentieth century. As they watched the rapidly growing technology of mass production collide with traditional patterns of management, they saw clearly that the resulting inefficiency was wasteful and appalling.

As the classical theorists began to examine the problems of management erupting in the production centers of society, they shaped notions about organizations that were intended to resolve many of the administrative ills within them. Many of the classical theorists' ideas on work and management were defined as universal scientific principles. If these principles were applied to almost any organizational

FIGURE 8.2 / The Evolution of Organization Theory

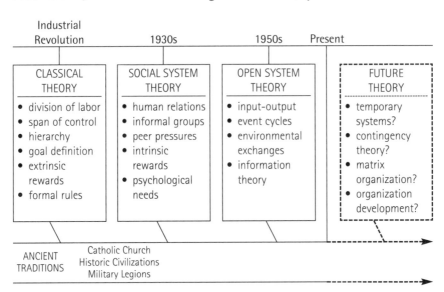

Industrial Revolution	1930s	1950s	Present
CLASSICAL THEORY	**SOCIAL SYSTEM THEORY**	**OPEN SYSTEM THEORY**	**FUTURE THEORY**
• division of labor • span of control • hierarchy • goal definition • extrinsic rewards • formal rules	• human relations • informal groups • peer pressures • intrinsic rewards • psychological needs	• input-output • event cycles • environmental exchanges • information theory	• temporary systems? • contingency theory? • matrix organization? • organization development?

ANCIENT TRADITIONS   Catholic Church / Historic Civilizations / Military Legions

Adapted from B. Hodge and H. Johnson, *Management and Organizational Behavior: A Multidimensional Approach* (New York: John Wiley & Sons, 1970), p. 19. Copyright © 1970 by John Wiley & Sons, Inc. Reprinted by permission of John Wiley & Sons, Inc.

setting, it was argued, the result would be the efficient use of time, materials, and personnel.

The classical theorists believed that an application of bureaucratic structure and processes or organizational control would promote rational, efficient, and disciplined behavior, making possible achievement of well-defined goals. Efficiency, then, is achieved by arranging positions within an organization according to hierarchy and jurisdiction, and by placing power at the top of a clear chain of command. Scientific procedures are used to determine this chain of command. Scientific procedures also are used to determine the best way of performing a task, and ten rules are formulated that require workers to perform in a prescribed manner. Experts are hired for defined roles and are grouped according to task specialization. Using rationally defined structures and processes such as these, a scientifically ordered flow of work can be carried out with maximum efficiency.

The conceptual model distilled from classical theory had a great impact on the practice and study of organizational life. It quickly spilled over the boundaries of industry and was incorporated into management practice in all sectors of society, including educational institutions (Exhibit 8.1).

Social Systems Theory

Within the classical theory framework the individual worker was conceived of as an object, a part of the bureaucratic machine. Preparing the work environment for maximizing labor efficiency was not unlike applying precepts from the physical sciences to the human domain of work. As Elton Mayo found in the Hawthorne Works' studies, the impact of social–psychological variables within a worker group was significant. The discovery that workers could control the production process to a considerable degree, independent of the demands of management, shattered many of the precepts central to classical theory. A new era of organization theory had arrived. This domain of thought is sometimes referred to as *social systems theory.*[3]

Classical management theory taught that the needs of the organization and the needs of the worker coincided—if the company prospered, the worker would prosper, as well. However, as an awareness of the basic differences between the needs of the individual and the needs of the organization grew, and as worker groups became more sophisticated in manipulating the production process, management technology gave birth to social systems theory and its approaches as a means of reducing conflict. The argument went that by being considerate, using democratic procedures whenever possible, and maintaining open lines of communication, management and workers could talk over their respective problems and resolve them in a friendly, congenial way.

Not unlike the classical theory of the previous generation, the

EXHIBIT 8.1 / Scientific Management Principles Applied to Schools

Scientific Management Principles	Adaptation to Education
Formation of a hierarchy with graded levels of authority	Levels of control: superintendent to assistant superintendent to principals to vice-principals to teachers to students.
Scientific measurement of tasks and levels of performance	Students thoroughly tested in subject areas, aptitude, and achievement and classified by levels of learning.
Shape unity of ends (of managers and workers)	Conventional wisdom in schools dictates that teachers and administrators have the same objective: doing what is best for kids.
Define a scientific order of work	Third-grade knowledge is differentiated and preparatory to fourth-grade knowledge, which is differentiated and preparatory to fifth-grade knowledge, and so on.
Establish a division of labor	English teachers, history teachers, coaches, teacher aides, janitors, administrators, and so on.
Determine appropriate span of control	Thirty elementary students per teacher, 20 high school students per teacher, four vice-principals per principal.
Adhere to the chain of command	Teachers must talk first with the principal before going to see the superintendent.
Define rules of behavior	Teachers' handbook: "All teachers will be in their rooms by 8:00 A.M. and are obligated to remain on the school premises until 3:30 P.M. Teachers will stand outside their rooms and monitor the passing of students between periods. A copy of all messages being sent by teachers to parents must be on file in the principal's office."

EXHIBIT 8.1 / Scientific Management Principles Applied to Schools
(continued)

Scientific Management Principles	Adaptation to Education
Establish discipline among the employees	Students will abide by the rules of the school and the norms of good conduct. Teachers will adhere to the policies of the district and the norms of the teaching profession.
Recruitment based on ability and technical knowledge	Teaching and/or administrative credential required for certification to enter the field.
Define the one best way of performing a task	Schools continually search for the best way of teaching reading, mathematics, history, and the like.

---

human relations orientation to the problems of managerial control quickly spread to other sectors of society, including schools. The social upheaval caused by the Depression and turmoil of World War II created a receptive climate for this new administrative theory. Enthusiasm for the human relations orientation dampened considerable after the 1950s, however, because many worker organizations came to view it as just another management tactic designed to exploit workers.

The study of behavior in social system settings intensified, however, and a greater sophistication developed about how and why group members behave as they do under given conditions. In time, a natural social systems orientation to the analysis of behavior evolved in the literature as an alternative to the rational systems approach. The natural social systems orientation attempts to take into account how people do behave in organizations rather than how they should behave.

The conceptual perspective of the natural social systems model suggests that an organization consists of a collection of groups (social systems) that collaborate to achieve system goals on some occasions and, on other occasions, that cooperate to accomplish the goals of their own groups. Coalitions among subgroups within an organization (e.g., English teachers, history teachers and social studies teachers) form to provide power bases on which action can be taken (e.g., "Let's all vote to reject writing behavioral objectives."). Within the social systems framework the study of formal and informal power is one of several critical variables used to identify and analyze the processes of organizational governance.

Open System Theory

During the 1960s, another strand of thought developed that originated in the new technostructure of society. The earlier two traditions of classical and social systems theory tend to view organizational life as a closed system—that is, as isolated from the surrounding environment. *Open system theory* sees an organization as a set of interrelated parts that interact with the environment. It receives inputs such as human and material resources, values, community expectations, and societal demands; transforms them through a production process (e.g., classroom activities); and exports the product (e.g., graduates, new knowledge, revised value sets) into the environment (e.g., businesses, the military, homes and colleges) with value added. The organization receives a return (e.g., community financial support in the form of school taxes or tuition) for its efforts so it can survive and prosper and begin the cycle over again.

Within the systems theory context, the organization is perceived as consisting of cycles of events that interlock through exporting and importing with other organizations, which also are made up of cycles of events. Management is very complex because leadership has almost no control over the shifting conditions in the environment (e.g., new laws, demographic shifts, political climate, market for graduates) on the input or the output side of the equation. Control of the production process is also complex because the various subsystems of the organization (e.g., athletic department or minority group students) also are shaped by event cycles that are programmed by values, expectations, traditions, and vested interests. Changing these internal subgroups and their event cycles is difficult. The administrator attempts to stream the cycles together so that minimum conflict and inefficiency is generated.

Through the perspective of open system theory, a new logic on issues of organizational governance has emerged. It emphasizes the relationship of the organization with its surrounding environment, and thus places a premium on planning and programming for events that cannot be controlled directly. The key to making an open system work effectively and efficiently is its ability to gather, process, and use information. In a school, then, the facility with which a need is discovered, a goal is established, and resources are coalesced to meet that need determines the effectiveness and efficiency of that school. This characteristic of the institution is particularly important if change is to take place effectively.

Contingency Theory

In recent years, a view of organization development has surfaced that treats each organization, and even entities within the organization, as unique. For centuries this orientation has been at the core of practitioner behavior but has been seen as an anomaly, reflective of inefficiency or unpreparedness (managing by the seat of your pants), and thus was overlooked by management scientists. Currently, the changing situational character of management is now coming to be understood as a key to the management process itself.

Many management scholars and practitioners would now agree with the observation that *contingency theory* is perhaps the most powerful current and future trend in organization development. At this stage of development, however, contingency theory is not really a theory. Rather, it is a conceptual tool that facilitates our understanding of the situational flow of events and alternate organizational and individual responses to that flow. Thus, as a conceptual tool, contingency theory does not possess the holistic character of the three major models discussed earlier. In many ways contingency theory can be thought of as a subset of open system theory because it is through open system theory that we come to understand the dynamic flows of events, personnel, and resources that take place in organizations. It is also helpful for understanding the process of change, and the need for the educational institution undergoing change to have facets of all three mainstream organizational structures. It is equally important that the change agent be aware of the organizational structure impact on whether the reform is ultimately successfully implemented.

Implementing the Plan

Once the organizational structure is in place, the next step in operationalizing the change is to devise and implement a plan of action. The reform project should be separated into a series of activities, with the complex activities being subdivided into elements or events, the completion of which will conclude the activity. Clearly defined responsibilities should be assigned and accepted. Before proceeding, there is need to establish realistic target dates, develop the project calendar, and put into place a monitoring and evaluation process. Project planning computer software is of great assistance in organizing and managing large projects.[4]

Change Management

Perhaps the ability to manage change can be enhanced by categorizing the change to be accomplished in one of three zones, according to the intensity of the change. In the first zone, *low intensity and complexity*, change comes through the normal management process. Principals and department chairs, for example, set goals, give assignments, and monitor performance as they normally would. In the next zone, *medium intensity and complexity*, the top leaders in the school district have to be involved, at least to the point of assigning responsibility of the change to a specific individual or group. Adopting a whole language reading approach might be an example of this type of reform. In the third zone, marked by the *greatest intensity and complexity*, the highest-ranked leader needs to take even day-to-day responsibility. If this transformational change is to take place, the leader and the senior staff become so personally involved that management of the reform consumes most of their time. Rightsizing and restructuring a school district could be an example of a third-level reform.

Establishing Target Dates

Establishing precise starting and completion times for the project as a whole, and for each of the separate project activities, is critical. To establish realistic completion dates, it is essential that those involved in the project understand: (a) the nuances of the reform; (b) certain organizational realities, and (c) the capabilities of the staff. If these conditions are met, then it is possible to set realistic target dates. To do this, the project team raises two questions: First, If unanticipated problems arise (e.g., strikes, inclement weather, budgeting problems), what is the most pessimistic date by which this reform could be implemented? and, second: If all goes well, what is the most optimistic date by which this project could be completed? The realistic target date is a point midway between these two dates.

Gantt Charting

Once the activities and tasks have been delineated, the specific element of the more complex activities detailed, and responsibilities assigned, the master schedule needs to be developed and posted. This is developed in the form of a Gantt chart. Figure 8.3 depicts a Gantt chart for operationalizing a new reading program.[5]

Collective Bargaining and Change

An often overlooked instrument of change is collective bargaining. Too often the labor agreement is looked upon exclusively as a document affecting salary and fringe benefits. However, working conditions is a legitimate collective bargaining area, and many reforms involve significant alteration of these conditions. Therefore, collective bargaining can be the occasion for educational reform.

A good example of a change being spawned, and then operationalized, in a bargaining agreement is the increased knowledge and use of technology by the faculty and staff. One is hard-pressed these days to pick up an educational journal without seeing abundant evidence of the urgency with which schools are embracing classroom technology. Concurrent with the explosion of schools seeking access to the Information Highway, many are beginning to recognize that the promise of classroom technology lies not in the capabilities of the hardware and software, but in the manner in which educators are able to transform their instructional practices. Without this recognition, districts run the risk that their investments in technology will result in nothing more than equipping their classrooms with computers that are underused.

In the Hilton School District, in suburban Rochester, New York, there were many of the same concerns as they embarked on their implementation of classroom technology. In developing a technology plan, they drew on the experiences of private industry. They observed that two of the most significant barriers to successful implementation are employee training and resistance to change. They sought to overcome these obstacles by using the collective bargaining process. They created a financial incentive that would motivate the teachers and staff to achieve a baseline level of technological competency.

The Hilton School District identified two key objectives in this area: (a) preserving existing staff development initiatives, and (b) encouraging teacher computer use. Thus, they provided a financial incentive in that at any time during the life of the negotiated agreement, a teacher who demonstrated proficiency with an agreed-upon set of computer competencies would be eligible for a $500 increase in base salary. Alternatively, a teacher qualifying for the incentive could elect to receive a one-time reimbursement of $1,200 toward the purchase of a home computer. The district would also facilitate the lease purchase of computers via payroll deduction with purchase plans established with major suppliers.[6]

FIGURE 8.3 / Improving Reading Skills at Hughes Middle School

#	Task Name	Duration	% Completed
1	Reading In-Service	0d	0.00%
10	New Teacher In-Service	20d	0.00%
9	Reading in the Subject Area	0d	0.00%
8	Language Arts	20d	0.00%
13	Science	20d	0.00%
14	Math	20d	0.00%
15	Social Studies	20d	0.00%
2	Reader of the Month	0d	0.00%
19	September Reader	20d	0.00%
16	October Reader	20d	0.00%
17	November Reader	20d	0.00%
11	December Reader	20d	0.00%
18	January Reader	20d	0.00%
3	Volunteers Program	220d	0.00%
12	Parent Director	5d	0.00%
4	After-School Study Program	200d	0.00%
5	"Why I Read"	100d	0.00%
6	"Here's an Author"	100d	0.00%
7	Storytelling Time	100d	0.00%

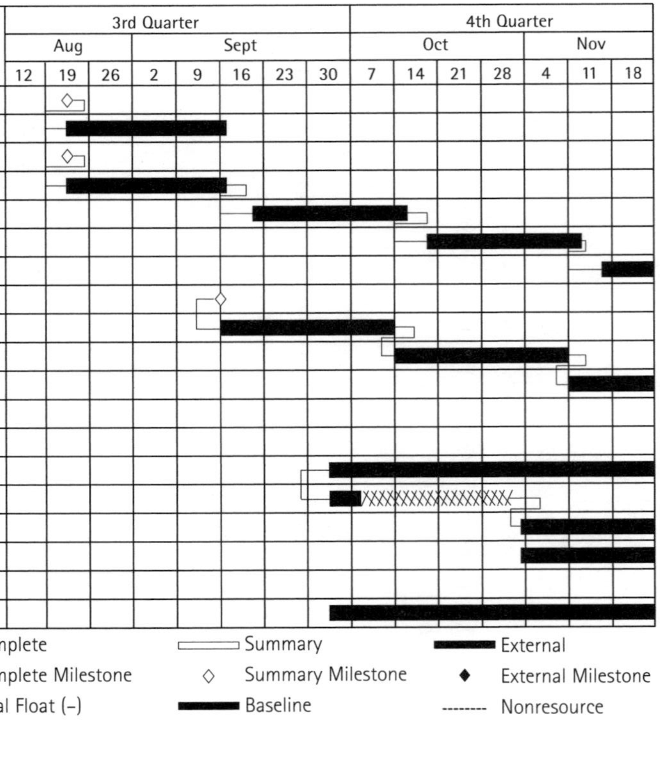

The first-year results exceeded the district's expectations. Eighty-seven percent of the eligible population achieved competency certification, and there was a 15 percent increase in those who owned or leased their own computers.

■ A CASE STUDY

Although our school system exhibited characteristics of all three models of organizational structure, it is basically organized according to the open system approach. We make extensive use of the matrix design where, depending on the task and function, a staff member could be reporting to two or three different supervisors. We find that such an arrangement stimulates effective communication and creativity. However, when communicating with our external constituencies, such as parents, business leaders, and, especially, the media, our staff was encouraged to use a classical communication structure and speak with one voice.

The ILA program fit into the existing organizational structure quite nicely. Educational programs had been organized according to a matrix model for at least ten years. Reading specialists, for example, report to the curriculum supervisors when dealing with curriculum and instruction, and to the assistant principal when communicating with parents via the parents' newsletter. Evaluation of a faculty member's performance is the purview of the curriculum supervisor, assistant principal, and principal, working collaboratively.

Other open systems characteristics include an external advisory committee, which keeps us in touch with the outside environment. Likewise, PTAs and Home and School Associations engender input and connection with the external environment.

Characteristics of the classical model of organization include (a) formal job descriptions; (b) educational standards for each program; (c) a formal assessment system for students, faculty and staff; and (d) a very structured governance and advisory system.

Social system organizational characteristics include (a) the teacher mentoring approach, (b) an ILA recognition program for both students and teachers, and (c) a constructivist (interactive) approach to instruction. By encompassing the best aspects of all of the organizational models, our school system was structured in such a way as to facilitate successful operationalizing of this change.

Diagnostic Checklist

Here are a few questions you can address in assessing your institution's readiness to operationalize a change:

1. Has the organizational structure of your institution been *analyzed?*
2. Is an appropriate organizational structure *in place?*
3. If not, can one be *developed?*
4. Are the *best aspects* of the various organizational models being used?
5. Are characteristics of the *open system* and the *contingency* models of organizational structure present?

Endnotes

1. Robert H. Palestini, *The Ten-Minute Guide to Educational Leadership* (Lancaster: Technomic Publishing, 1998).

2. Ibid., p. 10.

3. Ibid., p. 11.

4. Gerald C. Ubben and Larry W. Hughes, *The Principal* (Boston: Allyn and Bacon, 1996), p. 119.

5. Ibid., p. 119.

6. Steven V. Ayers, Collective bargaining as an instrument of change, *School Business Affairs* (February 9, 1998): 19–22.

9

Evaluating Change

It is no profit to have learned well,
if you neglect to do well.
— Publilius Syrus

Authentic assessment is a topical issue in education these days. Many are questioning exactly how to assess performance most accurately, effectively, and fairly, both human performance. After generations of focusing on program inputs, stressing program outcomes as an authentic measure of a program's effectiveness are gaining in popularity. This emphasis on outcomes should be applied to evaluation of a change or reform.

The change agent(s) should collect data about the nature and effectiveness of the change. The results of the evaluation indicate whether the change process is complete, or a return to an earlier stage should occur. The criteria for success should be specified in advance of a change effort. These criteria may be culturally linked and varied; they also should be closely related to the goals of the reform. If ineffective outcomes result from the introduction of site-based management, for example, the process should return to an earlier stage, such as assessment, to determine if the institution is really needed and the school community has been properly prepared for it.

Reform Outcomes

One process for evaluating the effectiveness of a change or reform is to consider participants' affective reactions, learning, behavior changes, and performance changes.[1]

Affective reactions are the participants' attitudes or disposition toward the reform. Questionnaires and interviews can be used to collect this information. Obviously, the change agent(s) is looking for development of a positive attitude toward the change. If it has been operationalized successfully, positive attitudes should prevail.

Learning refers to the participants' understanding of the change and the acquisition of new knowledge and skills as a result of its successful implementation. In the case of introducing cooperative learning techniques in the classroom, did the participants develop an understanding of the principles of cooperative learning, and do they demonstrate the skills needed to implement it properly in the classroom? Classroom observations are one way of assessing whether appropriate learning has taken place. If the staff development phase of the integrated change process has been implemented properly, appropriate learning should be apparent.

Behavioral changes include *participants'* actions in the workplace. Do they interact appropriately with colleagues and others? The following behavioral changes might occur as a result of an effectively implemented change:

- *Communicating openly.* Sharing intentions, motives, needs, feelings, and observations. Asking for and giving feedback that is descriptive rather than judgmental, and specific rather than general. Using active listening techniques, including paraphrasing, summarizing, asking for clarification, and checking out the observation of one's external behavior and attitude. Using assertive communication techniques, rather than being nonassertive or aggressive.
- *Collaborating.* Discussing, planning, and revising the goals of the reform jointly and cooperatively. Using participative decision-

making techniques, while avoiding arbitrary and unilateral decisions. Expanding influence skills so that compelling arguments for one's point of view can be made, rather than making decisions by fiat.

- *Taking responsibility.* Being a self-starter and not depending on constant direction. Taking the initiative to develop innovative and creative ways of performing one's duties. Streamlining the organization or department activities to promote operating efficiency.
- *Maintaining a shared vision.* Developing and communicating a clear philosophy, along with goals and objectives. Having and telling a story, a shared history that gives meaning to the institution's activities. Creating rituals and ceremonies to reestablish and remember values.
- *Solving problems effectively.* Defining problems in a nonadversarial way so that they may be resolved from a win/win perspective rather than win/lose. Perceiving and projecting problems as challenges rather than obstacles. Using group problem-solving techniques where applicable.
- *Respecting/supporting.* Using the various motivational theories to generate enthusiasm and give affirmation to and support for desired behavior. Dwelling on an individual's strengths, rather that on his or her weaknesses. Giving individuals the benefit of the doubt, and not being judgmental. Exhibiting ethical behavior and treating everyone fairly.
- *Processing/facilitating interactions.* Clarifying meeting goals and purposes. Reserving time at the end of meetings to critique what was done well/poorly, what facilitated making the decision or performing the task (a colleague of mine ends every meeting by asking each individual, "What did you learn today?"). While this can be annoying if overdone, it is an effective example of processing/facilitating interactions behavior.
- *Inquiring and experimenting.* Using an analytical approach to problem solving. In the process, looking for new and creative ways of addressing an issue. Frequently examining and questioning the

existing structure and culture to be certain they maximize the institution's goals.

The following are common behavior changes that educational *leaders* exhibit when a change or reform has been operationalized properly.

Generating participation. Involving other people when they have the necessary expertise, when the decision must be high quality, and when it also requires high acceptance. Relaxing traditional lines of command and empowering others to make decisions. Assuming a delegating, coaching style rather that a directive, task-oriented style.

Leading by vision. Continually articulating the institution's mission, goals, and objectives. Providing feedback mechanisms whereby faculty and staff *own* the institution's goals. Revising the institution's mission and the leader's personal vision when necessary.

Functioning strategically. Articulating underlying causes, interdependencies, and long-range consequences and acting accordingly. Acting in an institutional mode, rather than a territorial one. Developing strategies and tactics to operationalize the institution's mission and goals. Developing the faculty and staff knowledge and skills required to meet future objectives.

Promoting information flow. Communicating clearly the elements necessary to make the change effective. Being clear about expectations, commitments, and needs. Establishing multiple channels of communication and using the appropriate one under existing circumstances. Establishing the proper chain of command for the various types of communication. For example, external communication ordinarily should follow a formal chain of command, while internal communication may follow a less formal, or matrix line. Enhancing mechanisms for feedback.

Developing others. Teaching needed skills and preparing others within the institution to replace those who may leave. Rewarding desired behavior and delegating to those who prove ready and capable of increased responsibility. Providing opportunities for and building on employees' successes. Adapting one's leadership style to readiness level of the follower(s).

Evaluating Institutional Reform

In evaluating the effectiveness of an institutional reform and the process leading to the reform, an institution may address the following questions:[2]

- How did the institution determine the knowledge and skills necessary to implement the reform, and what type of staff development program was used to bring about the desired results?
- What were the conditions—economic, political, and demographic—of the external environment at the time of the reform?
- Did the conditions in the external environment have an effect on the success of the reform?
- How much has the institution's internal environment changed, and has it had an effect of the effectiveness of the reform.
- What are the primary technologies necessary to implement the reform?
- What is the prevailing structure and culture of the institution, and is it conducive to effecting change?
- Is the division of labor appropriate to implement the change effectively?
- What is the prevailing norm of the institution regarding improvement efforts?
- How comprehensive and consistent with current organization theory were the guiding assumptions and models used in implementing the reform?
- Were the purposes and need to implement the reform clear and accepted?
- Was a change process established, and were all of the steps used and integrated?

- Were the appropriate change agents identified and empowered?
- How explicit and detailed were the plans?
- What were the intended outcomes of the program, and what were the actual outcomes?
- How were the outcomes assessed?

The answers to these questions will enable the evaluator to assess whether the reform attained its objectives and, if it did not, determine the possible reasons.

■ A CASE STUDY

The success of the ILA program was determined in a number of ways, all of which were related to the goals of the program and were outcomes-based. For example, a longitudinal study will compare the long-term achievement of those exposed to the ILA program and their counterparts who preceded them. This assessment, of course, is consistent with the primary goal of the ILA program, to improve the school system's reading and language arts scores.

Other goals included continuous improvement of reading and language arts skills and improvement of both the students' cognitive development and their awareness of the way they learn (metacognition). Portfolio development was the method used to assess the progress students made in their writing skills. Journal writing and cognitive mapping also were used to assess the students' writing skills, but, just as important, these were used to assess their cognitive development.

A team made up of internal and external stakeholders has been established to monitor the evaluation. They have been charged with establishing an outcomes-based process for doing so. Input criteria, such as qualifications and number of faculty, computer technology, library resources, and student advising and mentoring, already have been established. Too often, we evaluate the success of programs based on these criteria. Although input criteria are important, authentic assessment deals primarily with outcomes. Will these ILA-trained students be properly prepared to perform the skills of reading and writing effectively? In other words, were the intended outcomes of the program realized? This is how a program should be evaluated.

Diagnostic Checklist

Here are a few questions you can address in assessing your institution's evaluation process:

1. Is an *evaluation process* an integral part of the change process?
2. Does the evaluation process use *authentic assessment* devices?
3. Is the evaluation process *outcomes-based*?
4. Are the outcomes related to the reform's *goals*?
5. Is there a mechanism for *revising* the reform if the evaluation outcomes indicate that revision is appropriate?

Endnotes

1. Judith R. Gordon, *A Diagnostic Approach to Organizational Behavior*, 4th Edition (Boston: Allyn and Bacon, 1993), p. 697.

2. Ibid., p. 701.

10

Institutionalizing Change

You can exert no influence if you are
not susceptible to influence.
— Carl Jung

Provided that the evaluation process shows that the reform has been
effective, the change then should become institutionalized—that is, the
changed processes should be established as permanent ways of operating. Otherwise, when the current change agent(s) leaves, the change
may not be perpetuated. Ideally, the reform should become part of the
organizational culture. It is in this way that a legacy is created from
which future generations of students, parents, faculty, and staff can
benefit. The results of a failure to institutionalize a reform are often
seen at the state and federal Department of Education levels. How
many times have we seen a governor or president set an educational
agenda, only to have it scuttled and replaced with a different agenda
by the subsequent administration? If a successful change is to prevail
over time, it must be institutionalized.

Thus, action must extend beyond short-term changes for real organizational improvement to take place. Enculturating the change
must be a significant goal of the integrated change process. How, for
example, does site-based management become a permanent part of
governance at Washington School? Certainly, the way the activities

are performed in moving from the first to the last step in the integrated change process will influence the permanency of the change. Accurate targeting of forces influencing change, followed by careful selection of change agents and intervention strategies, and concluding with effective action, contribute to long-range improvement.

In addition, mechanisms for continual monitoring of the changes must be developed and instituted. Permanent committees or task forces to observe ongoing implementation and outcomes can serve the monitoring functions. Formulation of new institutional policies and procedures based on the reform can encourage its continuation. Most important, however, is a commitment to the reform by the great majority of the school community. This community's commitment will expedite the reform's institutionalization.

Educational leaders, therefore, must build learning communities, ones that emphasize ongoing adaptability and self-generation, thereby emphasizing coping and looking at the world creatively. Peter Senge says, "Leaders in learning organizations are responsible for building organizations where people are continually expanding their capabilities to shape their future—that is, leaders are responsible for learning."[1] Where better to implement Senge's ideas regarding a learning community than in an educational institution?

Heroes and Storytellers

Another way of institutionalizing a reform is by encouraging development of heroes who embody the institution's vision and tribal storytellers who promulgate it. We often hear individuals in various organizations describe a colleague as "an institution around here." Heroes such as these do more to establish the organizational culture of an institution than any manual or policies and procedures handbook ever written. The senior faculty member who is recognized and respected for his or her knowledge and humane treatment of students is an invaluable asset to an educational institution. This person is a symbol of the institution's character. It is the presence of these heroes that sustains the reputation of the institution and allows the workforce to feel good about themselves and about the place where they work. The deeds and accomplishments of these heroes need to be promulgated to become part of the institution's folklore.

The deeds of these heroes usually are perpetuated by an organization's tribal storytellers, individuals who know the history of the institution and relate it through stories of its former and current heroes. An effective leader encourages the tribal storytellers, knowing that they are serving an invaluable service. They work at the process of institutional renewal, they allow the institution to improve continuously, they preserve and revitalize the values of the institution, and they mitigate the tendency of institutions, especially educational institutions, to become bureaucratic. Every institution has its heroes and storytellers. It is the educational leader's function to see to it that things like manuals and handbooks do not replace them.

One caveat regarding these heroes and storytellers, however, is that they can also perpetuate the status quo and thus be a force against change. The key is to let them know first of an impending change. If informed at the outset and convinced of the reform's efficacy, the heroes and storytellers can be among the change agent's most valuable assets throughout the process, especially during the institutionalization phase. Cultivation of heroes and storytellers needs to take place early in the process if they are to be an asset by the end of the process. This is another indication of the importance of considering this process as integrated, rather than step-by-step.

■ A CASE STUDY

The ILA program we have been using as our case study has not reached the institutionalization phase. However, the groundwork has been laid for successful institutionalization to take place. Provided that the evaluation process continues to show that expected outcomes are realized, our heroes and tribal storytellers are ready to go into action. They were the first to have been consulted about the efficacy of the ILA program, and their support was cultivated. As a result, they took *ownership* of the program and helped guide it through the development process. We are certain that once the program is judged to be a success, the heroes and storytellers will claim credit for the ILA program and perpetuate its continued existence. The old adage, "Success has many fathers, while failure is an orphan," comes immediately to mind in facilitation of the institutionalization process.

At any rate, the point is, to leave a legacy of successful reforms for your successors, the changes need to be institutionalized. In addition to the changes being incorporated into the institution's catalogs, manuals, and handbooks, the heroes and storytellers play an important role. Be certain to use all of these resources in institutionalizing an effective reform.

Diagnostic Checklist

Here are a few questions you can address in assessing whether your institution has institutionalized a reform:

1. Has the evaluation process indicated that the change has been *effective*?
2. Has the foundation been established by involving the *heroes and storytellers* early in the process?
3. Has the change been incorporated into the institution's *catalogs, manuals, and handbooks*?
4. Have the heroes and storytellers been encouraged to *do their part* in institutionalizing the change?

Endnotes

1. Peter M. Senge. The leader's new work: Building learning organizations, *Sloan Management Review* (Fall 1990): 7–23.

11

Schoolwide Reform Models

I don't care to be involved in the crash landing
unless I can be in on the takeoff.
— Harold Stassen

Previous chapters spoke of the steps that need to be taken to implement a significant educational reform effectively, using the implementation of an integrated language arts program as a model for bringing about a desired change. This chapter explores the merits of seven schoolwide reform models proposed by various scholars as possible solutions to some of the problems that seem to plague elementary and secondary education in the United States.

Theodore Sizer's Coalition of Essential Schools
Theodore Sizer was named dean of Harvard's Graduate School of Education at age thirty one. After almost eight years in that post, he became headmaster of Phillips Academy in Andover, Massachusetts. In 1981 Sizer left Andover to chair a large research project called, *A Study of High Schools*. Out of that experience came Horace's Compromise and the beginnings of the Coalition of Essential Schools. Sizer became convinced that every student could perform well if given the proper setting and support, that no two schools would be alike because no two school cultures were alike, and that shining the powerful light of intellectual

inquiry on complex problems could lead to new questions and possible solutions. The Coalition started at Brown University in 1984 as a small effort working with five or ten schools that would operate around a set of *Nine Common Principles*, including these four: the purpose of the school is to help students think; exhibitions are superior to tests because they help you and the student see what the youngster really knows; you teach best when you know your students well, so no secondary teacher should see more than eighty students each day; and students learn best when they believe what they are learning is important.

The Nine Common Principles have not changed over the intervening years of their application, but the magnitude of the program has. The Coalition now includes almost one thousand schools in thirty-eight states and two foreign countries. These schools are public and private, wealthy and poor. Most are secondary schools, although more elementary schools join each year. More than one-third of the students in Coalition schools are from minority groups. There is also considerably more emphasis on giving families and students a choice about where to go to school. Wealthy families have always had a choice; not so for poor families.

It has been demonstrated that choice can work in public schools in East Harlem, New York. There, if a school is successful, its program is duplicated in another school. If the school fails, it is closed. Under the current system, Sizer argues, ineffective schools have no incentive to improve. But there can be several small schools inside a single building, and an individual school can be dissolved and a new one started on the same site. Children gain nothing if support continues for schools that consistently fail. Schools, according to Sizer, should enroll no more than a few hundred students, and the ratio of staff to students must allow for a high degree of personalization.

Sizer attributes the Coalition's success to the understanding that effective schools are unique. The Coalition's approach is not cookie-cutter. To be effective, a school has to reflect its own community. Therefore, no particular model is imposed on a school or school system. Sizer's research indicates that significant, long-term reform is only achieved with subtle but powerful support and collaboration among teachers, students, and families of the students in a particular community. Absent that, short-term changes in instruction are possible, but not long-term results. This means that important decisions have to be made by the people most affected. This frustrates researchers who want to look at how this design works in practice, because each community does things in it own fashion. But Sizer believes that each school has to look at reform in its own particular way.[1]

Personalized Learning

Developing academically responsive classrooms is important for a country built on the values of equity and excellence. Proponents of *personalized learning* argue that both of these goals can be met if we establish heterogeneous communities of learning built on high-quality curriculum and instruction that strive to maximize each student's potential.

A serious pursuit of differentiation, or personalized learning, causes us to reexamine our traditional ways of schooling. Is it reasonable to expect all students at a certain grade level to learn the same material? Can students learn more responsibly on an independent basis? Is cooperative learning of any value? Do we need to cover the material, or have children mastered what they can?

These questions are important, but they resist easy answers. In answering them, we can try various methods of differentiation. We can assign reading buddies to support the range of readers or develop a learning contract with several options for practicing math skills. Maybe we could try a tiered lesson or interest centers. Three students who clearly understand the chapter need an independent study project. But, the first step in making differentiation work is the hardest. We have to know where we want to end up before we start out, and we need to plan well how to get there—that is, we must have solid curriculum and instruction in place before we adapt them to each child's specific needs.

Suppose Teacher A is teaching about ancient Greece. The students are reading the textbook in class today. The teacher suggests that they take notes of important details as they read. When they finish, they answer the questions at the end of the chapter. Students who do not finish in class must do so for homework. Tomorrow, they will answer the questions together in class. The teacher likes to lecture and works hard to prepare his presentations. Students are expected to take copious notes. They know they will be quizzed on the notes and the text. They will receive a study sheet that clearly spells out what will be on the test.

Teacher B is also teaching about ancient Greece. The students are given graphic organizers to use as they read the textbook chapter, and the teacher goes over the organizers with the class so that anyone who missed details can fill them in. The teacher brings in examples of the art and architecture of the period and tells how important the Greeks were in shaping our civilization. When the teacher invites some students to dress in togas and act as Plato and Aristotle, someone suggests bringing in food so the class can have a typical Greek meal. On another day, they watch a movie clip that dramatizes Greek mythology. Later, the teacher reads aloud about the various Greek gods, and the students talk about what they learned last year about Greece. The students then go over the chapter together in small groups, which they like much better than working alone at home.

It would be easy to say that the Teacher A's class was not differentiated, and teacher B's class was. But, to have true personalized learning, there must be both student understanding and student engagement. One could argue that Teacher A's class had understanding, although it was based too much on memorization, while Teacher B's class had student engagement, but may have lacked student understanding. Teacher B could have developed a truly differentiated instruction by planning the year around a few key concepts that help students relate to, organize, and retain what they study in history. The teacher also could develop principles or generalizations that govern or uncover how the concepts work. Further, for each unit, the teacher could have established a defined set of facts and terms that are essential for students to know to be literate and informed about the topic. The teacher needs to list the skills for which the teacher and the students are responsible as the year progresses. Finally, the teacher has to develop essential questions to intrigue the students and engage them in a quest for understanding.

The effectively organized, personalized learning classroom plans for what students should know, understand, and be able to do at the end of a sequence of learning. It dignifies each learner by planning tasks that are interesting, relevant, and powerful. It invites each student to wonder. It determines where each student is in knowledge, skill, and understanding and where that student needs to move. It differentiates instruction to facilitate that goal. For the personalized learning teacher, differentiated instruction is one piece of the puzzle. It is not a strategy to be plugged in occasionally or often; it is a way of thinking about the classroom. There is what students learn, and how they learn it. Personalized learning has to do not so much with the *what* but with the *how*. We must remember, however, that if the *what* is ill-conceived, the how—in this case personalized learning—is doomed.[2]

The Constructivist Classroom

For years, the term *constructivism* appeared only in journals read primarily by scholars. Now, constructivism regularly appears in teacher's manuals for textbooks, state education department curriculum standards, education reform literature, and educational practitioner journals. In short, constructivism has reached the mainstream of educational thought.

Constructivism is a theory of learning that describes the central role the learner, versus the teacher, plays in transforming their mental schemes in their cognitive growth. Education, however, has deep roots in other theories of learning. This history constrains our capacity to embrace the central role of the learner in his or her own education.

Many educators believe that students learn on demand. This belief is manifested in the traditional scope and sequence of the typical course of study and, more recently, in new educational standards and assessments. This approach to schooling is grounded in the conviction that all students can learn the same material in the same time frame. For some students, this approach leads to the construction of knowledge, but for many it does not.

Teachers must adapt the adjust lessons on the basis of students' evolving needs. Constructivist educational practice cannot be realized without the classroom teacher's autonomous, ongoing, professional judgment. Furthermore, learners control their learning. This simple truth lies at the heart of the constructivist approach to education.

According to the constructivists, educators develop classroom practices and negotiate the curriculum to enhance the likelihood of student learning. But controlling what students learn is virtually impossible. The search for meaning takes a different route for each student. Even when educators structure classroom lessons and curricula to ensure that all students learn the same concepts at the same time, each student still constructs his or her own unique meaning through his or her own cognitive processes. In other words, as educators we have great control over what we teach, but far less control over what students learn.

Shifting our priorities from ensuring that all students learn the same concepts to ensuring that we analyze students' understandings carefully to customize our teaching approaches is an essential step in educational reform that results in increased learning. Again, teachers must set standards for their own professional practice and free students from the anti-intellectual training that occurs when teachers "teach to the test."

The five central tenets of constructivism are:

- Constructivist teachers seek and value students' points of view. Knowing what students think about concepts helps teachers formulate classroom lessons and differentiate instruction on the basis of students' needs and interests.

- Constructivist teachers structure lessons to challenge students' suppositions. All students, whatever their age, come to the classroom with life experiences that shape their views about how their world works. When educators permit students to construct knowledge that challenges their current suppositions, learning occurs. Only through asking students what they think they know, and why they think they know it, are teachers and students able to confront their suppositions.
- Constructivist teachers recognize that students must attach relevance to the curriculum. As students see relevance in their daily activities, their interest in learning grows.
- Constructivist teachers structure lessons around big ideas, not small bits of information. Exposing students to wholes first helps them determine the relevant parts as they refine their understandings of the wholes.
- Constructivist teachers assess student learning in the context of daily classroom investigations, not as separate events. Students demonstrate their knowledge every day in a variety of ways. Defining understanding as only that which is capable of being measured by paper-and-pencil assessments administered under strict security perpetuates false and counterproductive myths about academia, intelligence, creativity, accountability, and knowledge.

The following example demonstrates the constructivist approach to student-centered learning. A fourth-grade teacher returned a test from the previous day. Question 3 was, "There are 7 blue chips and 3 green chips in a bag. If you place your hand in the bag and pull out 1 chip, what is the probability that you will get a green chip?" One student wrote, "You probably won't get one." A nonconstructivist teacher might mark the answer wrong. A constructivist teacher not only would mark it correct, because it is, but also would ask the student what his or her thinking process was in arriving at the answer (usually referred to as *metacognition* or thinking of how we think).[4]

Standards–Based Education

The standards movement is a major force in educational reform today. The promise of *standards-based education* can be seen in several school districts throughout the country.[4]

- Fort Logan Elementary School in Denver, Colorado, where scores rose significantly when teams of teachers analyzed weaknesses in performance relative to grade-level standards. Each team reviewed test data and developed strategies for helping students learn in identified areas of difficulty.
- Lake Havasu City, Arizona, where teams of Title I teachers identified, defined, and focused instruction on common reading skills. Once teachers had a shared language about which skills to concentrate on, they improved strategies and systems to improve instructional quality and consistency. As a result, the number of students reading at or above grade level rose from 20 to 35 percent in just one year.
- Glendale Union High School District near Phoenix, Arizona, where teams of teachers have increased student performance for almost every course offered. All district teachers—whether they teach algebra, U.S. history, biology, or senior English—are teaching to the same year-end assessments developed by subject-area teams. The same coordination is happening at Adlai Stevenson High School in Lincolnshire, Illinois, where teacher teams continue to set measurable achievement records on every kind of assessment.

How did these school obtain these results? Not by focusing on standards contained in state or professional documents. Their efforts preceded those documents. Nonetheless, in each case, teachers knew exactly what students need to learn, what to teach to, where to improve, and what to work on with colleagues. Clear, common learning standards, manageable in number, promote better results. They are essential to focus and coherence.

The two basic questions before us are: Do we already have sufficiently clear standards? Are state and professional standards documents truly helping us achieve the focus and coherence that are vital to success? For advocates of standards-based education, the answer to both questions is no. So, what do we do?

Consider a school where teachers know exactly what essential skills and knowledge students should learn that year and where their colleagues are teaching to the same manageable standards. Because of this, their fellow teachers can collaborate with them on lessons and units.

This, in turn, leads to a living bank of proven, standards-referenced instructional materials—lessons, units, and assessments perfected through action research. Both new and veteran teachers can peruse these targeted materials, learning from and adding to the richness of the faculty's repertoire. Because of these rich resources, new and inexperienced teachers achieve confidence and competence much more rapidly, and experienced teachers have a sense of making a meaningful, ongoing contribution to their profession while being renewed by instructional ideas that engage students. Proven methods, practices, and lessons aligned with established standards become the center of the professional dialogue, and results on local, state, and formative assessments continually improve. Such an alignment leads inevitably to better results on local and state assessments and on norm-referenced, alternative, and criterion-referenced assessments.

To create this model in schools, the following steps are suggested:

1. Start with the standards that are assessed; be circumspect about those that are not assessed. After thoroughly reviewing the state standards, you may find that many of these will not be assessed fully. While educators are trying maniacally to cover all of the standards, many of them will disappear because of their own ir-

relevancy and imprecision. Concentrate only on the standards actually contained in current state and norm-referenced or criterion-referenced assessments.

2. Beyond state assessments, add judiciously to the list of standards you wish to teach. Because of the limitations of state and norm-referenced test, we must develop local and district standards and assessments that take us beyond them. Districts should review the standards documents, but then exercise severe discipline in prioritizing on the basis of what students will need most if they are to become reflective thinkers, competent workers, and responsible citizens. For every grade or level, pilot your new standards and assessments while asking the question: Are the standards clear, relevant, and not so numerous that they sacrifice depth over breadth?

3. Do not add more topics than can be taught and assessed reasonably and effectively. The tendency toward overload is strong in most schools and can be crippling to improvement efforts. At the local and state levels, economy and clarity must inform all standards, and standards must be aligned meaningfully with assessments. Every teacher deserves a clear, manageable, grade-by-grade set of standards and learning benchmarks that make sense and allow a reasonable measure of autonomy. Anything less is frustrating, inhumane, and counterproductive.

According to its proponents, well-thought-out standards-based education gives the desired results. But this requires a focused disciplined effort. The result will be a new coherence and a shared focus that could be the most propitious step to take toward educating all students well.v

Glasser's Control Theory

William Glasser suggests that individuals strive to gain control over their emotions and behavior so they will have healthier and more productive lives. His *control theory* posits that individuals are born with five basic human needs—survival, love, power, fun, and freedom—that must be satisfied for them to be productive in their work and private lives. According to Glasser, people need to control their own behavior so as to make the most need-satisfying choices possible. His definition of a quality school, and its attainment of excellence through his axioms is shown in figure 11.1.

The survival need is the innate desire of individuals to be safe and secure. Love refers to the need for affiliation and affirmation. Power is the need to obtain knowledge and expertise. To Glasser, knowledge is power. Our inalienable right to the pursuit of happiness is our effort to fulfill the need for fun. And the opportunity to make free choices is what Glasser believes satisfies our need for freedom.

According to Glasser, effective educational administrators see that these five needs are satisfied if the administrators expect their faculty and staff to be productive. In turn, faculty satisfy these needs in their students if they expect their students to be successful. Coercion and competition are counterproductive. Quality performance, therefore, cannot be achieved in an adversarial setting. Faculty, students, and staff will perform if coerced, but they *not* in a quality manner. Competition enables one person to succeed while others fail. Cooperation, on the other hand, allows many winners.

Although Glasser's control theory has not been verified by empirical research, it has been demonstrated successfully in a number of schools and school systems, most notably, the Johnson City, New York, school district. In Johnson City, an urban school system, standardized achievement test scores increased dramatically while Glasser's techniques were used. The faculty was also judged to be more productive when programs were implemented that satisfied the five basic needs.

In a systemwide movement, Glasser challenged both administrators and faculty to integrate into their programs and lesson plans ways of satisfying the five basic needs of survival, love, power, fun, and freedom. Teachers, for example, were expected to prepare their daily lesson plans by asking themselves in what specific ways the

FIGURE 11.1 / Glasser's Theory

CONTROL THEORY
People need to be able to control their own behavior so as to make the most need satisfying choices possible.

Basic Human Needs:
Survival
Love
Power
Fun
Freedom

THE QUALITY SCHOOL

DEFINITION: A school that . . .
- All students are doing high-quality work
- The teachers are ensuring that students' basic needs are met
- The principal is facilitating conditions that support what students and teachers need

AXIOMS:
- All behavior reflects one's attempts to satisfy basic needs
- Behavior problems are caused by students' resistance to work they perceive is unconnected to any of their basic needs
- In quality schools, students are workers whose job it is to produce quality work
- Teachers are "lead" rather than "boss" managers whose job it is to help students see how doing quality work will allows their basic needs to be met
- It is impossible for bored students to do quality work

Adapted from William Glasser, *Control Theory*, Harper & Row, 1989.

lesson was meeting the students' need for survival, love, power, fun, and freedom. By having every level of employee perform this exercise on a daily basis, Glasser was able to operationalize his control theory. The results speak for themselves. Glasser's model is differentiated further from the other schoolwide reform models mentioned here in that it is the only one so solidly based on a theoretical foundation. The advantage is that theory often can correct failed practice. If, for example, a particular lesson did not seem to be effective, the teacher could reflect on Glasser's control theory to see if one or more of the basic needs was not satisfied, and make needed revisions before that lesson was presented again. Thus, theory informs practice. On the other hand, if the lesson proves to be effective, this is an instance of practice informing or reinforcing theory.[6]

The Paideia Proposal

The Paideia Proposal was written by Mortimer Adler for the Paideia Group in 1982. The name *paideia* indicates the orientation of the group. Paideia comes from the Greek words *pias* and *paidos* related to pedagogy and pediatrics, and refers to the upbringing of children or the general learning all humans should possess. According to the Paideia Group, the nation's two great accomplishments of the twentieth century are compulsory, public education and extension of universal suffrage. The next great challenge facing democracy is to offer not only the same quantity of public schooling to all citizens, but the same quality as well. As the system is arranged now, some students are offered a broad education designed to train their minds, while others take unchallenging courses that lack academic content. Students on the academic track study the humanities, students on the vocational track are trained for jobs, and students on the general track are not prepared for much of anything. These divisions hobble democracy and unfairly determine the academic and social destiny of the young. Adler argues that tracking must be abolished. He faults the present system for assuming that some children are not educable for the duties of self-governing citizenship and contends that all but severely injured children are capable of enjoying the most precious products of the human mind.

The Paideia Proposal argues that schools should have the same three intellectual objectives for all students, without exception:

1. Students must be prepared to carry on learning after high school graduation. Schooling is the beginning of education, and it must prepare students for a life of learning.
2. Schooling must prepare students for full participation in a democratic society. It is not enough that citizens vote; they must possess habits of informed discretion so they can analyze issues, engage in debate, and vote intelligently.
3. Schools must prepare all citizens to earn a living.[7]

These three objectives are achieved, not through specialized study or vocational training, but through a general liberal education. The curriculum of a Paideia school includes: language, literature, and the fine arts; mathematics and natural science; history, geography, and social studies. Adler insists that all sidetrack specialized courses and elective choices must be eliminated.

Studies acknowledge that some students learn faster and easier than others and that some ultimately learn more than their classmates. Despite these differences, all children share the same human nature. All are capable of observing, inquiring, learning, thinking, and communicating, and all deserve the opportunity to develop these capabilities fully. Schools need to acknowledge these common characteristics by offering the same quality education to all.

According to the Paideia group, there are three ways in which the mind can be improved: (a) by acquisition of organized knowledge; (b) by development of intellectual skills; and (c) by enlargement of understanding, insight, and aesthetic appreciation (table 11.1).

The acquisition of organized knowledge involves didactic instruction. Students are introduced to organized knowledge through lectures, laboratory demonstrations, and textbooks. There is much evidence that many students today are not exposed to the rudimentary knowledge necessary to challenge their thinking and improve their minds.

It is not enough that students acquire knowledge, however. They need to acquire the reading, writing, speaking, listening, observing, measuring, estimating, and calculating skills. These skills are learned and improved, not by listening and reading, but by doing. Teachers must play the role of a coach when youngsters are practicing academic skills, give assignments that involve students, and monitor the students' work carefully so that errors can be corrected as they occur. Academic coaching is not unlike athletic coaching in this regard. Students are asked to go through an organized sequence of acts again and again until they achieve a measure of perfection.

The enlargement of understanding means that students must acquire

---

TABLE 11.1 / The Paideia Proposal's Three Distinct Modes of Teaching and Learning

Column One	Column Two	Column Three
Acquisition of organized knowledge	Development of intellectual skills and skills of learning	Enlarged understanding of ideas and values
by means of	*by means of*	*by means of*
Didactic instruction, lectures, and responses Textbook and other aids	Coaching exercises and supervised practice	Socratic questioning and active participation
in three areas of	*in the operations of*	*in the*
Subject matter: Language, literature and the fine arts, mathematics and natural science, history, geography, and social sciences	Reading, writing, speaking, and listening Calculating and problem solving Observing, measuring, and estimating Exercising critical judgment	Discussion of books (not textbooks) and other works of art and involvement in artistic activities—e.g., music, drama, and the visual arts

Reprinted with permission of Macmillan Publishing Company from *The Paideia Proposal* by Mortimer J. Adler. Copyright © 1982 by The Institute for Philosophical Research. *Note:* The three columns do not correspond to separate courses, nor is one kind of teaching and learning necessarily confined to any one course.

---

knowledge and skills, but they must do much more. If they are to become competent citizens, students must practice the skills of critical intelligence; they must learn to think for themselves. If teachers are to awaken the creative and inquisitive powers of their pupils, certain things are required. First, students must learn to think for themselves. Second, students must be introduced to the methods of inquiry. Third, they need to be trained to be analytical and to question the assumptions on which beliefs are based. Finally, they need to be able to synthesize information in order to draw valid and reasonable conclusions.[8]

Effective Schooling

All of the above reform models have their advocates and critics. A meaningful method of assessing their potential effectiveness may be by placing them before the mirror of the effective schools research findings.

In 1984 and again in 1990, the Northwest Regional Educational Laboratory published a synthesis of what has become know as the *effective schools research* conducted in the 1970s and early 1980s. This extensive body of research identified the characteristics of effective schools. These researchers spanned the country visiting schools that were acknowledged as being effective. They found that effective schools could be located in any community, even the most economically and culturally distressed. All of these schools, no matter their location, manifested the characteristics embodied in the following findings:

1. Teachers and students work together over time to extend and refine each learner's knowledge and skills. Through careful pre-planning, effective classroom management and instruction, positive teacher–student interactions, attention to equity issues, and regular assessment, teachers and students can achieve success.

2. The qualities of the school as a whole can either enhance or detract from the learning environment. Key factors in support of student success include efficient planning and clear goals, validated organization and management practices, strong leadership and continuous improvement, positive staff and student interactions, a commitment to educational equity, regular assessment, support programs, and positive relationships with parents and community members.

Granted, myriad and complex details need to be considered in implementing these findings. The schoolwide reform models suggested here contain many of the concepts and strategies suggested by the effective schools research findings. There is reason to believe, therefore, that if implemented properly, any one or a combination of these reforms would be effective in improving a school's academic program. However, the key to proper implementation is that the *Ten Steps to Educational Reform* be used.

Conclusion

I am convinced that any of the reform models discussed here can be effective. As we have shown, they all conform in one way or another to the effective schools research findings and to the Commission on the Restructuring of the American High School's recommendations. Therefore, they all have the empirical research foundation that indicates success. However, if a transformational leader who knows and practices the *Ten Steps to Educational Reform* is not present, the effort will be fruitless. Time and again, I have seen instances where a worthy reform effort was mismanaged and ultimately abandoned, not because the reform was flawed, but because it was not implemented properly.

By definition, all attempts at educational reform involve change. Properly implementing change is what *The Ten Steps to Educational Reform* is all about. To be successful, the educational leader needs to systematically follow the steps suggested in the integrated change process. He or she must have established a *climate* for change in the school and school system. The need for the change must be clearly established, and it needs to be accompanied by a sense of urgency that will motivate the school community to take the needed action. Favorable and opposing forces need to be assessed so that the appropriate intervention strategies can be formulated. A number of alternative solutions need to be developed, from which the best should be chosen. In all of these activities, participative decision making should be practiced so that everyone in the school community gains a sense of ownership in the change. Let us also not forget to provide the staff development opportunities that must accompany any significant reform. Finally, once the reform is operationalized and evaluated as a success, it must be institutionalized so that future generations of students and staff can benefit from it.

Endnotes

1. Mark F. Goldberg, interview with Theodor Sizer, *Phi Delta Kappan* (June 1996): 685–87.

2. Carol Ann Tomlinson, Mapping a route toward differentiated instruction, *Educational Leadership* (September 1999): 12–16.

3. David Perkins, The many faces of constructivism, *Educational Administration* (November 1999): 6–11.

4. Michael W. Apple, Educational reports and economic reality, *Excellence in Education*, 20 (1999): 102.

5. Mike Schmoker and Robert J. Marzano, Realizing the promise of standards-based education, *Educational Administration* (March 1999): 17–21.

6. William Glasser, *Control Theory* (New York: Harper & Row), 1984.

7. Rodman B. Webb and Robert R. Sherman, *Schooling and Society*, 2nd edition, (New York: Macmillan Publishing Co., 1989), pp. 568–75.

8. Robert H. Palestini, *Educational Administration: Leading with Mind and Heart* (Lancaster: Technomic Publishing, 1999).

A

Appendix

Change Facilitator Styles Inventory*

This inventory contains descriptions of principal behavior grouped by style. The items are drawn from actual research comparing more and less effective principals involved in school improvement. The inventory provides an opportunity for you to describe a principal you know (or perhaps yourself), and to compare your responses with the change facilitator styles of these principals.

Each item comprises three different descriptors of principal behavior. Using a total of ten points, distribute points among the three to indicate the extent to which each describes your principal's behavior. Record your responses on the score sheet provided.

*The items in this inventory were identified as a result of an extensive research program investigating the relationship between principal behavior and successful school improvement. This program was conducted at the Research and Development Center for Teacher Education, University of Texas, Austin. The items are from Gene E. Hail and William L. Rutherford, "Three Change Facilitator Styles: How Principals Affect Improvement Efforts," paper presented at the Annual Meeting of the American Educational Research Association, Montreal, April, 1983. Available from the RDCTE, Austin, TX, document number 3155. See also "Leadership Variables Associated with Successful School Improvement" (Austin, TX: RDCTE, 1983).

Appendix A

Score Sheet

Principal Behaviors		R	M	I	Totals
A. Vision	1.	____	____	____	10
	2.	____	____	____	10
	3.	____	____	____	10
B. Structuring the school as a workplace	4.	____	____	____	10
	5.	____	____	____	10
	6.	____	____	____	10
	7.	____	____	____	10
	8.	____	____	____	10
C. Structuring involvement with change	9.	____	____	____	10
	10.	____	____	____	10
	11.	____	____	____	10
	12.	____	____	____	10
	13.	____	____	____	10
	14.	____	____	____	10
D. Sharing responsibility	15.	____	____	____	10
	16.	____	____	____	10
	17.	____	____	____	10
E. Decision making	18.	____	____	____	10
	19.	____	____	____	10
	20.	____	____	____	10
F. Guiding and supporting	21.	____	____	____	10
	22.	____	____	____	10
	23.	____	____	____	10
	24.	____	____	____	10
	25.	____	____	____	10
	26.	____	____	____	10
G. Structuring his/her professional role	27.	____	____	____	10
	28.	____	____	____	10
	29.	____	____	____	10
	30.	____	____	____	10
	31.	____	____	____	10
	32.	____	____	____	10
	33.	____	____	____	10

Ten Steps to Educational Reform: Making Change Happen

Principal Behaviors	R	M	I	Totals
34.	____	____	____	10
35.	____	____	____	10
36.	____	____	____	10
37.	____	____	____	10
TOTALS				370

Score	Style Emphasis	
0 – 39	Very Low	
40 – 136	Low	R = Reactor
137 – 233	Medium	M = Manager
234 – 330	High	I = Initiator
331 – 370	Very High	

Change Facilitator Styles Inventory (CFSI)

Principal Behaviors		R	M	I
A. Vision	1.	Accepts district goals as school goals	Accepts district goals but makes adjustments at school level to accommodate particular needs of the school	Respects district goals but insists on goals for school that give priority to this school's student need
	2.	Future goals/direction of school are determined in response to district-level goals/priorities	Anticipates the instructional and management needs of school and plans for them	Takes initiative in identifying future goals and priorities for school and in preparing to meet them
	3.	Responds to teachers', students', and parents' interest in the goals of the school and the district	Collaborates with others in reviewing and identifying school goals	Establishes framework of expectations for the school and involves others in setting goals within that framework
B. Structuring the school as a workplace	4.	Maintains low profile relative to day-to-day operation of school	Very actively involved in day-to-day management	Directs the ongoing operation of the school with emphasis on instruction. through personal actions and clear designation of responsibility

Appendix A

Change Facilitator Styles Inventory (CFSI)

Principal Behaviors	R	M	I
	5. Grants teachers autonomy and independence, provides guide	Provides guidelines and expectations for teachers and students	Sets standards and expects high performance levels for teachers, students, and self
	6. Ensures that district and school policies are followed and strives to see that disruptions in the school day are minimal	Works with teachers, students, and parents to maintain effective operation of the school	First priority is the instructional program; personnel and collaborative efforts are directed at supporting that priority
	7. Responds to requests and needs as they arise in an effort to keep all persons involved with the school comfortable and satisfied	Expects all involved with the school to contribute to effective instruction and management in the school	Insists that all persons involved with the school give priority to teaching and learning
	8. Allows school norms to evolve over time	Helps establish and clarify norms for the school	Establishes, clarifies, and models norms for the school
C. Structuring involvement with change	9. Relies on information provided by other change facilitators, usually from outside the school, for knowledge of the innovation	Uses information from a variety of sources to gain knowledge of the innovation	Seeks out information from teachers, district personnel, and others to gain an understanding of the innovation and the changes required
	10. Supports district expectations for change	Meets district expectations for change	Accommodates district expectations for change and pushes adjustments and additions that will benefit his/her school

Ten Steps to Educational Reform: Making Change Happen

Change Facilitator Styles Inventory (CFSI)

Principal Behaviors	R	M	I
	11. Sanctions the change process and strives to resolve conflicts when they arise	Involved regularly in the change process, sometimes with a focus on management, and at other times with a focus on the impact of the change	Directs the change process in ways that lead to effective use by all teachers
	12. Expectations for teachers, relative to change, are given in general terms	Tells teachers that they are expected to use the innovation	Gives teachers specific expectations and steps regarding application of the change
	13. Monitors the change effort principally through brief, spontaneous conversations and unsolicited reports	Monitors the change effort through planned conversations with individuals and groups and from informal observations of instruction	Monitors the change effort through classroom observation, review of lesson plans, reports that reveal specific teacher involvement, and specific attention to the work of individual teachers
	14. May discuss with the teacher information gained through monitoring	Discusses information gained through monitoring with teacher in relation to teacher's expected behavior	Gives direct feedback to teacher concerned information gained through monitoring, which includes a comparison with expected behaviors and a plan for next steps, possibly including improvements
D. Sharing responsibility	15. Allows others to assume the responsibility for the change effort	Tends to do most of the intervening on the change effort but will share some responsibility	Will delegate to carefully chosen others some of the responsibility for the change effort
	16. Others who assume responsibility are more likely to be outside the school—e.g., district facilitators	Others who assume responsibility may come from within or from outside the school	Others who assume responsibility are likely to be from within the school

Appendix A

Change Facilitator Styles Inventory (CFSI)

Principal Behaviors	R	M	I
	17. Others who assume responsibility have considerable autonomy and independence in which responsibilities they assume and how they carry them out	Coordinates responsibilities and stays informed about how others are handling these responsibilities	First establishes which responsibilities will be delegated and how they are to be accomplished, then works with others and closely monitors the carrying out of tasks
E. Decision making	18. Makes decisions required for ongoing operation of the school as deadlines for those decisions approach	Actively involved in routine decision making relative to instructional and administrative affairs	Handles routine decisions through established procedures and assigned responsibilities, thereby requiring minimal time
	19. Makes decisions influenced by the immediate circumstances of the situation and formal policies	Makes decisions based on the norms and expectations that guide the school and the management needs of the school	Makes decisions based on the standard of high expectations and what is best for the school as a whole, particularly learning outcomes and longer-term goals
	20. Willingly allows others to participate in decision making or to make decisions independently	Allows others to participate in decision making but maintains control of the process through personal involvement	Allows others to participate in decision making and delegates decision making to others within carefully established parameters of established goals and expectations
F. Guiding and supporting	21. Believes teachers are professionals and leaves them alone to do their work unless they request assistance or support	Believes teachers are a part of the total faculty and establishes guidelines for all teachers to be involved with the change effort	Believes teachers are responsible for developing the best possible instruction, so expectations for their involvement with innovation is clearly established

Ten Steps to Educational Reform: Making Change Happen

Change Facilitator Styles Inventory (CFSI)

Principal Behaviors	*R*	*M*	*I*
22. Responds quickly to requests for assistance and support in a way that is satisfying to the requester	Monitors the progress of the change effort and attempts to anticipate needed assistance and resources	Anticipates the need for assistance and resources and provides support as needed as well as sometimes in advance of potential blockages
23. Checks with teachers to see how things are going and to maintain awareness of any major problems	Maintains close contact with teachers involved in the change effort in an attempt to identify things that might be done to assist teachers with the change	Collects and uses information from a variety of sources to be aware of how the change effort is progressing and to plan interventions that will increase the probability of a successful, quality implementation
24. Relies on whatever training is available with the innovation to aid in the development of teacher's knowledge and skill relative to the innovation	In addition to the regularly provided assistance, seeks out and uses sources within and outside the school to develop teacher knowledge and skills	Provides increased knowledge or skill needed by the teachers through possible use of personnel and resources within the building
25. Provides general support for teachers as persons and as professionals	Provides support to individuals and to subgroups for specific purposes related to the change and to provide for their personal welfare	Provides direct programmatic support through interventions targeted to individuals and to the staff as a whole
26. Tries to minimize the demands of the change effort on teachers	Moderates demands of the change effort to protect teachers' perceived overload	Keeps ever-present demands on teachers for effective implementation

Change Facilitator Styles Inventory (CFSI)

Principal Behaviors	R	M	I
G. Structuring her/his professional role	27. Sees role as administrator	Sees role as avoiding or minimizing problems so instruction may occur	Sees role as one of ensuring the school has a strong instructional program with teachers teaching students so they are able to learn
	28. Believes others will generate the initiative for any school improvement that is needed	Engages others in regular review of school situation to avoid any reduction in school effectiveness	Identifies areas in need of improvement and initiates action for change
	29. Relies primarily on others for introduction of new ideas into the school	Is alert to new ideas and introduces them to faculty or allows others in the school to do so	Sorts through new ideas presented from within and from outside the school and implements those deemed to have high promise for school improvement
	30. Is concerned with how others view him/her	Is concerned with how others view the school	Is concerned with how others view the impact of the school on students
	31. Accepts the rules of the district	Lives the the rules of the district, but goes beyond minimum expectations	Respects the rules of the district, but determines behavior by what is required for maximum school effectiveness
	32. Opinions and concerns of others determine what will be accomplished and how	Is consistent in setting and accomplishing tasks and does much of it herself/himself	Tasks determined and accomplished are consistent with school priorities but responsibility can be delegated to others
	33. Maintains a general sense of "where the school is" and of how teachers are feeling about things	Is well informed about what is happening in the school and who is doing what	Maintains specific knowledge of all that is going on in the school through direct contact with the classroom, individual teachers, and students

Ten Steps to Educational Reform: Making Change Happen

Change Facilitator Styles Inventory (CFSI)

Principal Behaviors	*R*	*M*	*I*
34. Responds to others in a manner intended to please them	Responds to others in a way that is supportive of the operation of the school	Responds to others with concern, but places student priorities above all else
35. Develops minimal knowledge of what use of the innovation entails	Becomes knowledgeable about general use of the innovation and what is needed to support its use	Develops sufficient knowledge about use to be able to make specific teaching suggestions and to troubleshoot any problems that may emerge
36. Indefinitely delays having staff do tasks if perceives that staff are overloaded	Contends that staff are already very busy and paces requests and task loads accordingly	Will knowingly sacrifice short-term feelings of staff if doing a task now is necessary for the longer-term goals of the school
37. Ideas are offered by each staff member, but one or two have dominant influence	Some ideas are offered by staff and some by the principal; then consensus is developed gradually.	Seeks teachers' ideas and their reactions to her/his ideas; then priorities are set

B

Appendix

The Heart Smart Organizational Diagnosis Model

Just as there are vital signs by which to measure individual health, so are there vital signs by which to measure organizational institutions. This survey helps to determine those vital signs. The purpose of the Heart Smart Organizational Diagnosis Questionnaire is to provide feedback data for intensive diagnostic efforts. Use of the questionnaire, either by itself or in conjunction with other information-collecting techniques such as systematic observation or interviewing, provides the data needed to identify strengths and weaknesses in the functioning of an educational institution or school system.

A meaningful diagnostic effort must be based on a theory or model of organizational development. This makes action research possible because it facilitates problem identification, which is essential to determining the proper functioning of an organization. The model suggested here establishes a systematic approach for analyzing relationships among the variables that influence how an organization is managed. It provides for assessment of ten areas of formal and informal activity: structure, culture, leadership, motivation, communication, decision making, conflict resolution, goal setting and planning, power distribution, and attitude toward change. The circle in figure A.1 represents an organizational boundary for diagnosis. This boun-

FIGURE A.1 / Organizational Components

dary demarcates the functioning of the internal and external environments. The underlying organizational theory which this survey is based is an open systems model, so it is essential that influences from both the internal and external environment be considered for the analysis to be complete.

Appendix B

Please think of your **present work environment** and indicate the degree to which you agree or Disagree with each of the following statements. A "1" is *Disagree Strongly* and a "7" is *Agree Strongly*.

	DISAGREE STRONGLY	DISAGREE	DISAGREE SLIGHTLY	NEITHER AGREE NOR DISAGREE	AGREE SLIGHTLY	AGREE	AGREE STRONGLY
1. The manner in which the tasks in this institution are divided is logical.	1	2	3	4	5	6	7
2. The relationships among coworkers are harmonious.	1	2	3	4	5	6	7
3. This institution's leadership efforts result in its fulfilling of its purposes.	1	2	3	4	5	6	7
4. My work at this institution offers me an opportunity to grow as a person.	1	2	3	4	5	6	7
5. I can always talk to someone at work if I have a work-related problem.	1	2	3	4	5	6	7
6. The faculty actively participates in decisions.	1	2	3	4	5	6	7
7. There is little evidence of unresolved conflict in this institution.	1	2	3	4	5	6	7
8. There is a strong fit between this institution's mission and my own values.	1	2	3	4	5	6	7
9. The faculty and staff are represented on most committees and task forces.	1	2	3	4	5	6	7
10. Staff development routinely accompanies any significant changes that occur in this institution.	1	2	3	4	5	6	7
11. The manner in which the tasks in this institution are distributed is fair.	1	2	3	4	5	6	7
12. Older faculty's opinions are valued.	1	2	3	4	5	6	7
13. The administrators display the behaviors required for effective leadership.	1	2	3	4	5	6	7
14. The rewards and incentives here are both internal and external.	1	2	3	4	5	6	7
15. There is open and direct communication among all levels of this institution.	1	2	3	4	5	6	7
16. Participative decision making is fostered at this institution.	1	2	3	4	5	6	7
17. What little conflict exists at this institution is not dysfunctional.	1	2	3	4	5	6	7

	DISAGREE STRONGLY	DISAGREE	DISAGREE SLIGHTLY	NEITHER AGREE NOR DISAGREE	AGREE SLIGHTLY	AGREE	AGREE STRONGLY
18. Representatives of all segments of the school community participate in the strategic planning process.	1	2	3	4	5	6	7
19. The faculty and staff have an appropriate voice in the operation of this institution.	1	2	3	4	5	6	7
20. This institution is not resistant to constructive change.	1	2	3	4	5	6	7
21. The division of labor in this organization helps its efforts to reach its goals.	1	2	3	4	5	6	7
22. I feel valued by this institution.	1	2	3	4	5	6	7
23. The administration encourages an appropriate amount of participation in decision making.	1	2	3	4	5	6	7
24. Faculty and staff members are recognized often for special achievements.	1	2	3	4	5	6	7
25. There are no significant barriers to effective communication at this institution.	1	2	3	4	5	6	7
26. When the acceptance of a decision is important, a group decision-making model is used.	1	2	3	4	5	6	7
27. There are mechanisms at this institution to manage conflict and stress effectively.	1	2	3	4	5	6	7
28. Most of the employees understand the mission and goals of this institution.	1	2	3	4	5	6	7
29. The faculty and staff feel empowered to make their own decisions regarding their daily work.	1	2	3	4	5	6	7
30. Tolerance toward change is modeled by the administration of this institution.	1	2	3	4	5	6	7
31. The various grade level teachers and departments work well together.	1	2	3	4	5	6	7
32. Differences among people are accepted.	1	2	3	4	5	6	7
33. The leadership is able to generate continuous improvement in the institution.	1	2	3	4	5	6	7

Appendix B

34. My ideas are encouraged, recognized, and used. 1 2 3 4 5 6 7

35. Communication is carried out in a nonaggressive style. 1 2 3 4 5 6 7

36. In general, the decision-making process is effective. 1 2 3 4 5 6 7

37. Conflicts usually are resolved before they become dysfunctional. 1 2 3 4 5 6 7

38. For the most part, the employees of this institution feel an "ownership" of its goals. 1 2 3 4 5 6 7

39. The faculty and staff are encouraged to be creative in their work. 1 2 3 4 5 6 7

40. When changes are made, they are made within a rational process. 1 2 3 4 5 6 7

41. This institution's organizational design responds well to changes in the internal and external environment 1 2 3 4 5 6 7

42. The teaching and the nonteaching staffs get along with one another. 1 2 3 4 5 6 7

43. The leadership of this institution espouses a clear educational vision. 1 2 3 4 5 6 7

44. The goals and objectives for the year are developed mutually by the faculty and the administration. 1 2 3 4 5 6 7

45. I believe that my opinions and ideas are listened to. 1 2 3 4 5 6 7

46. Usually, a collaborative style of decision making is used at this institution. 1 2 3 4 5 6 7

47. A collaborative approach to conflict resolution ordinarily is used. 1 2 3 4 5 6 7

48. This institution has a clear educational vision. 1 2 3 4 5 6 7

49. The faculty and staff can express their opinions without fear of retribution. 1 2 3 4 5 6 7

/ 145 /

	DISAGREE STRONGLY	DISAGREE	DISAGREE SLIGHTLY	NEITHER AGREE NOR DISAGREE	AGREE SLIGHTLY	AGREE	AGREE STRONGLY
50. I feel confident that I will have an opportunity for input if a significant change is to take place in this institution.	1	2	3	4	5	6	7
51. This institution is people-oriented.	1	2	3	4	5	6	7
52. Administrators and faculty have mutual respect for one another.							
53. Administrators give people the freedom to do their job.	1	2	3	4	5	6	7
54. The rewards and incentives at this institution are designed to satisfy a variety of individual needs.	1	2	3	4	5	6	7
55. The opportunity for feedback is always available in the communications process.	1	2	3	4	5	6	7
56. Group decision-making techniques, such as brainstorming and group surveys, sometimes are used in the decision-making process.	1	2	3	4	5	6	7
57. Conflicts often are prevented by early intervention.	1	2	3	4	5	6	7
58. This institution has a strategic plan for the future.	1	2	3	4	5	6	7
59. Most administrators here use the power of persuasion rather than the power of coercion.	1	2	3	4	5	6	7
60. This institution is committed to continual improvement through the process of change.	1	2	3	4	5	6	7
61. This institution does not adhere to a strict chain of command.	1	2	3	4	5	6	7
62. This institution exhibits grace, style, and civility.	1	2	3	4	5	6	7
63. The administrators model desired behavior.	1	2	3	4	5	6	7

	DISAGREE STRONGLY	DISAGREE	DISAGREE SLIGHTLY	NEITHER AGREE NOR DISAGREE	AGREE SLIGHTLY	AGREE	AGREE STRONGLY
64. At this institution, employees normally are not coerced into doing things.	1	2	3	4	5	6	7
65. I have the information I need to do a good job.	1	2	3	4	5	6	7
66. I can challenge the decisions in this institution constructively.	1	2	3	4	5	6	7
67. A process to resolve work-related grievances is available.	1	2	3	4	5	6	7
68. There is an ongoing planning process at this institution.	1	2	3	4	5	6	7
69. The faculty and staff have input into the operation of this institution through a collective bargaining unit or through a faculty governance body.	1	2	3	4	5	6	7
70. The policies, procedures, and programs of this institution are reviewed periodically.	1	2	3	4	5	6	7

Heart Smart Scoring Sheet

Instructions: Transfer the numbers you circled on the questionnaire to the blanks below. Add each column and divide each sum by seven. This will give you comparable scores for each of the ten areas.

Structure	Culture	Leadership	Motivation
1____	2____	3____	4____
11____	12____	13____	14____
21____	22____	23____	24____
31____	32____	33____	34____
41____	42____	43____	44____
51____	52____	53____	54____
61____	62____	63____	64____

Total

____ ____ ____ ____

Average

____ ____ ____ ____

Communication	Decision Making	Conflict Resolution	Goal Setting/ Planning
5____	6____	7____	8____
15____	16____	17____	18____
25____	26____	27____	28____
35____	36____	37____	38____
45____	46____	47____	48____
55____	56____	57____	58____
65____	66____	67____	68____

Total

____ ____ ____ ____

Average

____ ____ ____ ____

Power Distribution	Attitude toward Change
9___	10___
19___	20___
29___	30___
39___	40___
49___	50___
59___	60___
69___	70___

Total

___   ___   ___   ___

Average

___   ___   ___   ___

The Heart Smart Organizational Diagnosis Interpretation Sheet

Instructions: Transfer your average scores from the Scoring Sheet to the appropriate boxes in the figure below. Then study the background information and interpretation suggestions that follow.

Interpretation and Diagnosis

A crucial consideration is the diagnosis based upon data interpretation. The simplest diagnosis would be to assess the amount of variance for each of the ten variables in relation to a score of 4, which is the neutral point. Scores *below* 4 would indicate a *problem* with organizational functioning. The closer the score is to 1, the more severe the problem would be. Scores *above* 4 indicate the *lack of a problem*, with a score of 7 indicating optimum functioning.

Another diagnostic approach follows the same guidelines of assessment in relation to the neutral point (score) of 4. The score of each of the seventy items on the questionnaire can be reviewed to produce more exacting information on problematic areas. Thus, diagnosis would be more precise. For example, let us suppose that the average score on item number 8 is 1.4. This would indicate not only a problem in organizational purpose or goal setting, but also a more specific problem in that there is a gap between organizational and individual goals. This more precise diagnostic effort is likely to lead to a more appropriate intervention in the organization than the generalized diagnostic approach described in the preceding paragraph.

Appropriate diagnosis must address the relationships between the boxes to determine the interconnectedness of problems. For example, if there is a problem with *communication*, could it be that the organizational *structure* does not foster effective communication. This might be the case if the average score on item 25 was well below 4 (2.5 or lower) and all the items on organizational *structure* (1, 11, 21, 31, 41, 51, 61) averaged above 5.5).

Index

A
Adler, Mortimer, 126

B
best practices, 50, 59
brainstorming, 60

C
change facilitator styles
  inventory, Appendix A, 14
classical organizational theory,
  90
coalition of essential schools,
  114
collective bargaining, 98
congruence model, 14
consensus mapping, 65
contingency theory, 96
continuous improvement, 17
control theory, 123
creative thinking, 65

D
decision making, 13, 58, 73, 75
Delphi technique, 23, 63
Deming, Edwards, 17

E
effective schools research, 129
employee ownership, 112
empowerment, 77
evaluating change, 103

F
force field analysis, 45, 50

G
Gantt charting, 98
garbage can model, 27, 58
Glasser, William, 123
Greenleaf, Robert, 10

H
Hanson, Mark E., 8

Hawthorne effect, 44
Heart Smart, Appendix B, 24
heroes and storytellers, 111

I
institutionalizing change, 110
Integrated Language Arts (ILA),
    17, 37, 55, 69, 79, 101, 108,
    112

L
lowerarchy, 44

M
mentoring, 85

N
Nadler, David, 14
National Diffusion Network, 18
A Nation at Risk, 47
needs assessment, 22
needs assessment instrument, 25
nominal group technique, 23, 61

O
open systems theory, 95
operationalizing change, 88
Organizational Climate Descrip-
    tion Questionnaire, 27
Organizational Health Inventory,
    27

P
Paideia Proposal, 126
paradigm shift, 89
personalized learning, 116
Pupil-Control Ideology Form, 27

R
resistance cycle, 41
resistance to change, 40, 47, 48,
    54

S
satisfice, 57
A School of Excellence, 35
Sizer, Theodore, 114
social systems theory, 92
staff development, 81, 82
standards-based education, 121
stress, stage of, 33
success syndrome, 35

T
Ten at Ten program, 18
Total Quality Management, 17
trust and respect, 10, 73

V
vision, 11
Vroom/Yetton decision-making
    model, 75

W
whole language model, 30

About the Author

Dr. Robert H. Palestini is currently dean of the Graduate School at Saint Joseph's University in Philadelphia. He is also a professor in the education department, specializing in educational administration and leadership. Dr. Palestini spent over thirty years in basic education, serving as a secondary school teacher, principal, assistant superintendent, and superintendent of schools. He has presented nationally on the topic of educational administration and has written three other books on various aspects of educational leadership.